Instructor's Manual to Accompany FUNDAMENTAL METHODS OF MATHEMATICAL ECONOMICS

Third Edition

ALPHA C. CHIANG
Professor of Economics
The University of Connecticut

McGraw-Hill Book Company
New York St. Louis San Francisco Auckland Bogotá Hamburg
London Madrid Mexico Montreal New Delhi Panama
Paris São Paulo Singapore Sydney Tokyo Toronto

Instructor's Manual to Accompany
FUNDAMENTAL METHODS OF MATHEMATICAL
ECONOMICS / Third Edition

ISBN: 0-07-010814-5

23 HAM/HAM 0 9 8 7 6 5 4 3

Printer/Binder: Greyden Press

CONTENTS

CHAPTER 2

Exercise 2.3

1 (a) $\{x \mid x > 27\}$ (b) $\{x \mid 8 < x < 73\}$

2 True statements: (d), (f), (g), and (h).

3 (a) $\{2,4,6,7\}$ (b) $\{2,4,6\}$ (c) $\{2,6\}$

(d) $\{2\}$ (e) $\{2\}$ (f) $\{2,4,6\}$

4 All are valid.

5 First part: $A \cup (B \cap C) = \{4,5,6\} \cup \{3,6\} = \{3,4,5,6\}$; and

$(A \cup B) \cap (A \cup C) = \{3,4,5,6,7\} \cap \{2,3,4,5,6\} = \{3,4,5,6\}$ too.

Second part: $A \cap (B \cup C) = \{4,5,6\} \cap \{2,3,4,6,7\} = \{4,6\}$; and

$(A \cap B) \cup (A \cap C) = \{4,6\} \cup \{6\} = \{4,6\}$ too.

7 $\emptyset$, $\{a\}$, $\{b\}$, $\{c\}$, $\{a,b\}$, $\{a,c\}$, $\{b,c\}$, $\{a,b,c\}$

8 There are $2^4 = 16$ subsets: $\emptyset$, $\{1\}$, $\{3\}$, $\{5\}$, $\{7\}$, $\{1,3\}$, $\{1,5\}$, $\{1,7\}$, $\{3,5\}$, $\{3,7\}$, $\{5,7\}$, $\{1,3,5\}$, $\{1,3,7\}$, $\{1,5,7\}$, $\{3,5,7\}$, and $\{1,3,5,7\}$.

9 The complement of U is $\tilde{U} = \{x \mid x \notin U\}$. Here, the notion of "not in U" is expressed via the $\notin$ symbol which relates an element (x) to a set (U). In contrast, when we say "$\emptyset$ is a subset of U," the notion of "in U" is expressed via the $\subset$ symbol which relates a subset ($\emptyset$) to a set (U). Hence, we have two different contexts, and there exists no paradox at all.

Exercise 2.4

1 (a) $\{(3,a), (3,b), (6,a), (6,b), (9,a), (9,b)\}$

(b) $\{(a,m), (a,n), (b,m), (b,n)\}$

(c) $\{(m,3), (m,6), (m,9), (n,3), (n,6), (n,9)\}$

2 $\{(3,a,m), (3,a,n), (3,b,m), (3,b,n), (6,a,m), (6,a,n), (6,b,m), (6,b,n), (9,a,m), (9,a,n), (9,b,m), (9,b,n)\}$

3 No. When $S_1 = S_2$.

4 None of these is a function, because there exist more than one y value for each given x value.

5 Range = $\{y \mid 8 \le y \le 17\}$

6 The range is the set of all nonpositive real numbers.

Exercise 2.5

2 Eqs. (a) and (b) differ in the sign of the coefficient of x; a positive (negative) sign means an upward (downward) slope.

Eqs. (a) and (c) differ in the constant term; a larger constant means a higher vertical intercept.

3 A negative coefficient (say, -1) for the x^2 term is associated with a hill. As the value of x is steadily increased or reduced, the $-x^2$ term will exert a more dominant influence in determining the value of y. Being negative, this term serves to pull down the y values at the two extreme ends of the curve.

4 If negative values can occur, there will appear in quadrant III a curve which is the mirror image of the one in quadrant I.

5 (a) x^{19} (b) x^{a+b+c} (c) $(xyz)^3$

6 (a) x^6 (b) $x^{1/6}$

7 By Rules VI and V, we can successively write $x^{m/n} = (x^m)^{1/n} = \sqrt[n]{x^m}$; by the same two rules, we also have $x^{m/n} = (x^{1/n})^m = (\sqrt[n]{x})^m$.

8 Rule VI: $(x^m)^n = \underbrace{x^m \times x^m \times \cdots \times x^m}_{n \text{ terms}} = \underbrace{x \times x \times \cdots \times x}_{mn \text{ terms}} = x^{mn}$

Rule VII: $x^m \times y^m = \underbrace{x \times x \times \cdots \times x}_{m \text{ terms}} \times \underbrace{y \times y \times \cdots \times y}_{m \text{ terms}}$

$$= \underbrace{(xy) \times (xy) \times \cdots \times (xy)}_{m \text{ terms}} = (xy)^m$$

CHAPTER 3

Exercise 3.2

1 (a) By substitution, we get $24 - 2P = -5 + 7P$, or $9P = 29$. Thus $\overline{P} = 3\frac{2}{9}$. Substituting $\overline{P}$ into the second or the third equation, we find $\overline{Q} = 17\frac{5}{9}$.

(b) With $a = 24$, $b = 2$, $c = 5$, $d = 7$, the formulas yield:

$$\overline{P} = \frac{29}{9} = 3\frac{2}{9}; \qquad \overline{Q} = \frac{158}{9} = 17\frac{5}{9}.$$

2 (a) $\overline{P} = \frac{61}{9} = 6\frac{7}{9}$; $\qquad \overline{Q} = \frac{276}{9} = 30\frac{2}{3}$.

(b) $\overline{P} = \frac{36}{7} = 5\frac{1}{7}$; $\qquad \overline{Q} = \frac{138}{7} = 19\frac{5}{7}$.

4 If $b + d = 0$, then $\overline{P}$ and $\overline{Q}$ in (3.4) and (3.5) would involve division by zero, which is undefined.

5 If $b + d = 0$, then $d = -b$, and the demand and supply curves would have the same slope (though different vertical intercepts). The two curves would be parallel, with no equilibrium intersection point in Fig. 3.1.

Exercise 3.3

1 (a) $\overline{x}_1 = 5$; $\overline{x}_2 = 2$. (b) $\overline{x}_1 = 4$; $\overline{x}_2 = -2$.

2 (a) $\overline{x}_1 = 5$; $\overline{x}_2 = 2$. (b) $\overline{x}_1 = 4$; $\overline{x}_2 = -2$.

3 (a) $(P - 1)(P + 5) = 0$; thus $\overline{P}_1 = 1$, and $\overline{P}_2 = -5$.

(b) $(x - 2)(x + 2)(x + 2) = 0$; thus $\overline{x}_1 = 2$, and $\overline{x}_2 = \overline{x}_3 = -2$.

(c) $(x - 4)(x - 1)(x - 2) = 0$; thus $\overline{x}_1 = 4$, $\overline{x}_2 = 1$, and $\overline{x}_3 = 2$.

(d) $x(x - 4)(x + 1) = 0$; thus $\overline{x}_1 = 0$, $\overline{x}_2 = 4$, and $\overline{x}_3 = -1$.

4 $(x - 7)(x + 2)(x - 5) = 0$, or $x^3 - 10x^2 + 11x + 70 = 0$.

5 (a) The model reduces to $P^2 + 6P - 7 = 0$. By the quadratic formula, we have $\overline{P}_1 = 1$ and $\overline{P}_2 = -7$, but only the first root is acceptable. Substituting that root into the second or the third equation, we find $\overline{Q} = 2$.

(b) The model reduces to $2P^2 - 10 = 0$, or $P^2 = 5$, with the two roots $\overline{P}_1 = \sqrt{5}$ and $\overline{P}_2 = -\sqrt{5}$. Only the first root is admissible, and it yields $\overline{Q} = 3$.

6 Equation (3.7) is the equilibrium condition stated in the form of "the excess supply be zero."

Exercise 3.4

2 $$\overline{P}_1 = \frac{(a_2 - b_2)(\alpha_0 - \beta_0) - (a_0 - b_0)(\alpha_2 - \beta_2)}{(a_1 - b_1)(\alpha_2 - \beta_2) - (a_2 - b_2)(\alpha_1 - \beta_1)}$$

$$\overline{P}_2 = \frac{(a_0 - b_0)(\alpha_1 - \beta_1) - (a_1 - b_1)(\alpha_0 - \beta_0)}{(a_1 - b_1)(\alpha_2 - \beta_2) - (a_2 - b_2)(\alpha_1 - \beta_1)}$$

3 Since we have

$c_0 = 18 + 2 = 20$ $\quad$ $c_1 = -3 - 4 = -7$ $\quad$ $c_2 = 1$

$\gamma_0 = 12 + 2 = 14$ $\quad$ $\gamma_1 = 1$ $\quad$ $\gamma_2 = -2 - 3 = -5$

it follows that

$$\overline{P}_1 = \frac{14 + 100}{35 - 1} = \frac{57}{17} = 3\frac{6}{17} \quad \text{and} \quad \overline{P}_2 = \frac{20 + 98}{35 - 1} = \frac{59}{17} = 3\frac{8}{17}$$

Substitution into the given demand or supply function yields

$$\overline{Q}_1 = \frac{194}{17} = 11\frac{7}{17} \quad \text{and} \quad \overline{Q}_2 = \frac{143}{17} = 8\frac{7}{17}$$

Exercise 3.5

1 (a) Three variables are endogenous: Y, C, and T.

(b) By substituting the third equation into the second, and then the second into the first, we obtain

$$Y = a - bd + b(1 - t)Y + I_0 + G_0$$

or $[1 - b(1 - t)]Y = a - bd + I_0 + G_0$

Thus $$\overline{Y} = \frac{a - bd + I_0 + G_0}{1 - b(1 - t)}$$

Then it follows that the equilibrium values of the other two endogenous variables are

$$\overline{T} = d + t\overline{Y} = \frac{d(1 - b) + t(a + I_0 + G_0)}{1 - b(1 - t)}$$

and $$\overline{C} = \overline{Y} - (I_0 + G_0) = \frac{a - bd + b(1 - t)(I_0 + G_0)}{1 - b(1 - t)}$$

2 (a) The endogenous variables are Y, C and G.

(b) $g = G/Y$ = proportion of national income spent as government expenditure.

(c) Substituting the last two equations into the first, we get

$$Y = a + b(Y - T_0) + I_0 + gY$$

Thus $$\overline{Y} = \frac{a - bT_0 + I_0}{1 - b - g}$$

(d) The restriction $b + g \neq 1$ is needed to avoid division by zero.

3 Upon substitution, the first equation can be reduced to the form

$$Y - 6Y^{1/2} - 55 = 0, \text{ or}$$

$$w^2 - 6w - 55 = 0 \qquad (\text{where } w \equiv Y^{1/2})$$

The latter is a quadratic equation, with roots

$$\overline{w}_1, \overline{w}_2 = \frac{1}{2}[6 \pm (36 + 220)^{1/2}] = 11, -5$$

From the first root, we can get

$$\overline{Y} = \overline{w}_1^{\,2} = 121 \qquad \text{and} \qquad \overline{C} = 25 + 6(11) = 91$$

On the other hand, the second root is inadmissible, because it leads to a negative value for $\overline{C}$:

$$\overline{C} = 25 + 6(-5) = -5$$

CHAPTER 4

Exercise 4.1

1 $Q_d - Q_s = 0$

$Q_d + bP = a$

$Q_s - dP = -c$

Coefficient matrix:

$$\begin{bmatrix} 1 & -1 & 0 \\ 1 & 0 & b \\ 0 & 1 & -d \end{bmatrix}$$

Vector of constants:

$$\begin{bmatrix} 0 \\ a \\ -c \end{bmatrix}$$

2 $Q_{d1} - Q_{s1} = 0$

$Q_{d1} - a_1P_1 - a_2P_2 = a_0$

$Q_{s1} - b_1P_1 - b_2P_2 = b_0$

$Q_{d2} - Q_{s2} = 0$

$Q_{d2} - \alpha_1P_1 - \alpha_2P_2 = \alpha_0$

$Q_{s2} - \beta_1P_1 - \beta_2P_2 = \beta_0$

Coefficient matrix:

$$\begin{bmatrix} 1 & -1 & 0 & 0 & 0 & 0 \\ 1 & 0 & 0 & 0 & -a_1 & -a_2 \\ 0 & 1 & 0 & 0 & -b_1 & -b_2 \\ 0 & 0 & 1 & -1 & 0 & 0 \\ 0 & 0 & 1 & 0 & -\alpha_1 & -\alpha_2 \\ 0 & 0 & 0 & 1 & -\beta_1 & -\beta_2 \end{bmatrix}$$

Variable vector:

$$\begin{bmatrix} Q_{d1} \\ Q_{s1} \\ Q_{d2} \\ Q_{s2} \\ P_1 \\ P_2 \end{bmatrix}$$

Constant vector:

$$\begin{bmatrix} 0 \\ a_0 \\ b_0 \\ 0 \\ \alpha_0 \\ \beta_0 \end{bmatrix}$$

Exercise 4.2

1 (a) $\begin{bmatrix} 4 & 2 \\ 9 & 7 \end{bmatrix}$ (b) $\begin{bmatrix} 4 & 4 \\ 0 & -8 \end{bmatrix}$ (c) $\begin{bmatrix} 12 & -3 \\ 18 & 27 \end{bmatrix}$ (d) $\begin{bmatrix} 20 & 18 \\ 24 & -6 \end{bmatrix}$

2 (a) Yes. $AB = \begin{bmatrix} 28 & 64 \\ 6 & 0 \\ 13 & 8 \end{bmatrix}$. No, not conformable.

(b) Both are defined, but $BC = \begin{bmatrix} 14 & 4 \\ 69 & 30 \end{bmatrix} \neq CB = \begin{bmatrix} 20 & 16 \\ 21 & 24 \end{bmatrix}$.

3 Yes. $BA = \begin{bmatrix} -\frac{1}{5} + \frac{12}{10} & 0 & -\frac{3}{5} + \frac{6}{10} \\ -3 + \frac{1}{5} + \frac{28}{10} & 1 & -2 + \frac{3}{5} + \frac{14}{10} \\ \frac{2}{5} - \frac{4}{10} & 0 & \frac{6}{5} - \frac{2}{10} \end{bmatrix} = \begin{bmatrix} 1 & 0 & 0 \\ 0 & 1 & 0 \\ 0 & 0 & 1 \end{bmatrix}$.

Thus we happen to have AB = BA in this particular case.

4 (a) $\begin{bmatrix} 0 & 1 \\ 36 & 20 \\ 16 & 3 \end{bmatrix}$ (3×2) (b) $\begin{bmatrix} 49 & 5 \\ 12 & 1 \end{bmatrix}$ (2×2) (c) $\begin{bmatrix} 3x + 2y \\ 4x+2y-7z \end{bmatrix}$ (2×1)

(d) $[7a+c \quad 2b+4c]$ (1×2)

5 (a) $x_2 + x_3 + x_4 + x_5$ (b) $a_5x_5 + a_6x_6 + a_7x_7 + a_8x_8$

(c) $b(x_1 + x_2 + x_3 + x_4)$

(d) $a_1x^0 + a_2x^1 + \ldots + a_nx^{n-1} = a_1 + a_2x + a_3x^2 + \ldots + a_nx^{n-1}$

(e) $x^2 + (x + 1)^2 + (x + 2)^2 + (x + 3)^2$

6 (a) $\sum_{i=1}^{3} ix_i\,(x_i - 1)$ (b) $\sum_{i=2}^{4} a_i(x_{i+1} + i)$ (c) $\sum_{i=1}^{n} \frac{1}{x^i}$ (d) $\sum_{i=0}^{n} \frac{1}{x^i}$

7 (a) $(\sum_{i=0}^{n} x_i) + x_{n+1} = x_0 + x_1 + \ldots + x_n + x_{n+1} = \sum_{i=0}^{n+1} x_i$

(b) $$\sum_{j=1}^{n} ab_jy_j = ab_1y_1 + ab_2y_2 + \ldots + ab_ny_n$$
$$= a(b_1y_1 + b_2y_2 + \ldots + b_ny_n) = a\sum_{j=1}^{n} b_jy_j$$

(c) $$\sum_{j=1}^{n}(x_j + y_j) = (x_1 + y_1) + (x_2 + y_2) + \ldots + (x_n + y_n)$$
$$= (x_1 + x_2 + \ldots + x_n) + (y_1 + y_2 + \ldots + y_n)$$
$$= \sum_{j=1}^{n} x_j + \sum_{j=1}^{n} y_j$$

Exercise 4.3

1 (a) $uv' = \begin{bmatrix} 5 \\ 2 \\ 3 \end{bmatrix} [3 \quad 1 \quad 9] = \begin{bmatrix} 15 & 5 & 45 \\ 6 & 2 & 18 \\ 9 & 3 & 27 \end{bmatrix}$

(b) $uw' = \begin{bmatrix} 5 \\ 2 \\ 3 \end{bmatrix} [7 \quad 5 \quad 8] = \begin{bmatrix} 35 & 25 & 40 \\ 14 & 10 & 16 \\ 21 & 15 & 24 \end{bmatrix}$

(c) $xx' = \begin{bmatrix} x_1 \\ x_2 \\ x_3 \end{bmatrix} [x_1 \quad x_2 \quad x_3] = \begin{bmatrix} x_1^2 & x_1x_2 & x_1x_3 \\ x_2x_1 & x_2^2 & x_2x_3 \\ x_3x_1 & x_3x_2 & x_3^2 \end{bmatrix}$

(d) $v'u = [3 \quad 1 \quad 9] \begin{bmatrix} 5 \\ 2 \\ 3 \end{bmatrix} = [15 + 2 + 27] = [44] = 44$

(e) $u'v = [5 \quad 2 \quad 3] \begin{bmatrix} 3 \\ 1 \\ 9 \end{bmatrix} = [15 + 2 + 27] = 44$

(f) $w'x = [7 \quad 5 \quad 8] \begin{bmatrix} x_1 \\ x_2 \\ x_3 \end{bmatrix} = [7x_1 + 5x_2 + 8x_3] = 7x_1 + 5x_2 + 8x_3$

(g) $u'u = [5 \quad 2 \quad 3] \begin{bmatrix} 5 \\ 2 \\ 3 \end{bmatrix} = [25 + 4 + 9] = [38] = 38$

(h) $x'x = [x_1 \quad x_2 \quad x_3] \begin{bmatrix} x_1 \\ x_2 \\ x_3 \end{bmatrix} = [x_1^2 + x_2^2 + x_3^2] = \sum_{i=1}^{3} x_i^2$

2 (a) All are defined except w'x and x'y'.

(b) $xy' = \begin{bmatrix} x_1 \\ x_2 \end{bmatrix} [y_1 \quad y_2] = \begin{bmatrix} x_1y_1 & x_1y_2 \\ x_2y_1 & x_2y_2 \end{bmatrix}$

$y'y = [y_1 \quad y_2] \begin{bmatrix} y_1 \\ y_2 \end{bmatrix} = y_1^2 + y_2^2$

$zz' = \begin{bmatrix} z_1 \\ z_2 \end{bmatrix} [z_1 \quad z_2] = \begin{bmatrix} z_1^2 & z_1z_2 \\ z_2z_1 & z_2^2 \end{bmatrix}$

$$yw' = \begin{bmatrix} y_1 \\ y_2 \end{bmatrix} [3 \quad 2 \quad 16] = \begin{bmatrix} 3y_1 & 2y_1 & 16y_1 \\ 3y_2 & 2y_2 & 16y_2 \end{bmatrix}$$

$x \cdot y = x_1 y_1 + x_2 y_2$

3 (a) $\sum_{i=1}^{n} P_i Q_i$

(b) Let P and Q be the column vectors of prices and quantities, respectively. Then the total cost is $P \cdot Q$, or $P'Q$, or $Q'P$.

4 (a) $w_1'w_2 = 11$ (acute angle, Fig. 4.3c)

(b) $w_1'w_2 = -11$ (obtuse angle, Fig. 4.3d)

(c) $w_1'w_2 = -13$ (obtuse angle, Fig. 4.3b)

(d) $w_1'w_2 = 0$ (right angle, Fig. 4.4)

(e) $w_1'w_2 = 5$ (acute angle, Fig. 4.4)

5 (a) $2v = \begin{bmatrix} 0 \\ 6 \end{bmatrix}$ (b) $u + v = \begin{bmatrix} 5 \\ 4 \end{bmatrix}$ (c) $u - v = \begin{bmatrix} 5 \\ -2 \end{bmatrix}$

(d) $v - u = \begin{bmatrix} -5 \\ 2 \end{bmatrix}$ (e) $2u + 3v = \begin{bmatrix} 10 \\ 11 \end{bmatrix}$ (f) $4u - 2v = \begin{bmatrix} 20 \\ -2 \end{bmatrix}$

6 (a) $4e_1 + 7e_2$ (b) $15e_1 - 2e_2 + e_3$

(c) $-e_1 + 3e_2 + 9e_3$ (d) $2e_1 + 8e_3$

7 (a) $d = \sqrt{(3-0)^2 + (2+1)^2 + (8-5)^2} = \sqrt{27}$

(b) $d = \sqrt{(9-2)^2 + 0 + (4+4)^2} = \sqrt{113}$

8 When u, v, and w all lie on a single straight line.

9 Let the vector v have the elements $(a_1, \ldots, a_n)$. The point of origin has the elements $(0, \ldots, 0)$. Hence:

(a) $d(0, v) = d(v, 0) = \sqrt{(a_1 - 0)^2 + \ldots + (a_n - 0)^2}$

$= \sqrt{a_1^2 + \ldots + a_n^2}$

(b) $d(v, 0) = (v'v)^{1/2}$ [See example 3 in this section.]

(c) $d(v, 0) = (v \cdot v)^{1/2}$

Exercise 4.4

1 (a) $(A + B) + C = A + (B + C) = \begin{bmatrix} 5 & 17 \\ 11 & 17 \end{bmatrix}$

(b) $(A + B) - C = A + (B - C) = \begin{bmatrix} -1 & 9 \\ 9 & -1 \end{bmatrix}$

2 No. It should be $A - B = -B + A$.

3 $(AB)C = A(BC) = \begin{bmatrix} 250 & 68 \\ 75 & 55 \end{bmatrix}$

4 (a) $k(A + B) = k[a_{ij} + b_{ij}] = [ka_{ij} + kb_{ij}] = [ka_{ij}] + [kb_{ij}]$

$= k[a_{ij}] + k[b_{ij}] = kA + kB$

(b) $(g + k)A = (g + k)[a_{ij}] = [(g + k)a_{ij}] = [ga_{ij} + ka_{ij}]$

$= [ga_{ij}] + [ka_{ij}] = g[a_{ij}] + k[a_{ij}] = gA + kA$

5 $(A + B)(C + D) = (A + B)C + (A + B)D = AC + BC + AD + BD$

6 No, $x'Ax$ would then contain cross-product terms $a_{12}x_1x_2$ and $a_{21}x_1x_2$. But the associative law would still apply.

Exercise 4.5

1 (a) $AI_3 = \begin{bmatrix} -1 & 8 & 7 \\ 0 & -2 & 4 \end{bmatrix} \begin{bmatrix} 1 & 0 & 0 \\ 0 & 1 & 0 \\ 0 & 0 & 1 \end{bmatrix} = \begin{bmatrix} -1 & 8 & 7 \\ 0 & -2 & 4 \end{bmatrix}$

(b) $I_2A = \begin{bmatrix} 1 & 0 \\ 0 & 1 \end{bmatrix} \begin{bmatrix} -1 & 8 & 7 \\ 0 & -2 & 4 \end{bmatrix} = \begin{bmatrix} -1 & 8 & 7 \\ 0 & -2 & 4 \end{bmatrix}$

(c) $I_2x = \begin{bmatrix} 1 & 0 \\ 0 & 1 \end{bmatrix} \begin{bmatrix} x_1 \\ x_2 \end{bmatrix} = \begin{bmatrix} x_1 \\ x_2 \end{bmatrix}$

(d) $x'I_2 = [x_1 \quad x_2] \begin{bmatrix} 1 & 0 \\ 0 & 1 \end{bmatrix} = [x_1 \quad x_2]$

2 (a) $Ab = \begin{bmatrix} -9 + 48 + 0 \\ 0 - 12 + 0 \end{bmatrix} = \begin{bmatrix} 39 \\ -12 \end{bmatrix}$

(b) AIb gives the same result as in (a).

(c) $x'IA = [-x_1 \quad 8x_1 - 2x_2 \quad 7x_1 + 4x_2]$

(d) x'A gives the same result as in (c).

3 (a) 4 × 3 (b) 2 × 6 (c) 4 × 1 (d) 2 × 5

4 The given diagonal matrix, when multiplied by itself, gives another diagonal matrix with diagonal elements $a_{11}^2, a_{22}^2, \ldots, a_{nn}^2$. For idempotency, we must have $a_{ii}^2 = a_{ii}$ for every i. Hence each a_{ii} must be either 1, or 0. Since each a_{ii} can thus have two possible values, and since there are altogether n of these a_{ii}, we are able to construct a total of 2^n idempotent matrices of the diagonal type. Two examples would be I_n and 0_n.

Exercise 4.6

1 $A' = \begin{bmatrix} 2 & -1 \\ 4 & 3 \end{bmatrix}$, $B' = \begin{bmatrix} 3 & 0 \\ 8 & 1 \end{bmatrix}$, $C' = \begin{bmatrix} 1 & 6 \\ 0 & 1 \\ 9 & 1 \end{bmatrix}$

2 (a) $(A + B)' = A' + B' = \begin{bmatrix} 5 & -1 \\ 12 & 4 \end{bmatrix}$ (b) $(AC)' = C'A' = \begin{bmatrix} 26 & 17 \\ 4 & 3 \\ 22 & -6 \end{bmatrix}$

3 Let $D \equiv AB$. Then $(ABC)' \equiv (DC)' = C'D' = C'(AB)' = C'(B'A')$ $= C'B'A'$.

4 $DF = \begin{bmatrix} 1 & 0 \\ 0 & 1 \end{bmatrix}$, thus D and F are inverses of each other. Similarly,

$EG = \begin{bmatrix} 1 & 0 \\ 0 & 1 \end{bmatrix}$, so E and G are inverses of each other.

5 Let $D \equiv AB$. Then $(ABC)^{-1} \equiv (DC)^{-1} = C^{-1}D^{-1} = C^{-1}(AB)^{-1}$ $= C^{-1}(B^{-1}A^{-1}) = C^{-1}B^{-1}A^{-1}$.

6 (a) A and X'X must be square, say n × n; X only needs to be n × m, where m is not necessarily equal to n.

(b) $AA = [I - X(X'X)^{-1}X'][I - X(X'X)^{-1}X']$

$= II - IX(X'X)^{-1}X' - X(X'X)^{-1}X'I + X(X'X)^{-1}X'X(X'X)^{-1}X'$

[see Exercise 4.4-5]

$$= I - X(X'X)^{-1}X' - X(X'X)^{-1}X' + XI(X'X)^{-1}X' \quad \text{[by (4.8)]}$$

$$= I - X(X'X)^{-1}X'$$

$$= A$$

Thus A satisfies the condition for idempotency.

CHAPTER 5

Exercise 5.1

1 (a) (5.2) (b) (5.2) (c) (5.3) (d) (5.3) (e) (5.3) (f) (5.1)

(g) (5.2)

(a) $p \Rightarrow q$ (b) $p \Rightarrow q$ (c) $p \Leftrightarrow q$

(a) Yes. (b) Yes. (c) Yes. (d) No; $v_2' = -2v_1'$.

We get the same results as in the preceding problem.

Exercise 5.2

(a) -6 (b) 0 (c) 0 (d) 157 (e) $3abc - a^3 - b^3 - c^3$

(f) $8xy + 2x - 30$

+, -, +, -, -.

$|M_a| = \begin{vmatrix} e & f \\ h & i \end{vmatrix}$ $|M_b| = \begin{vmatrix} d & f \\ g & i \end{vmatrix}$ $|M_f| = \begin{vmatrix} a & b \\ g & h \end{vmatrix}$

$|C_a| = |M_a|$ $|C_b| = -|M_b|$ $|C_f| = -|M_f|$

4 (a) 72 (b) -81

5 The cofactor of element 9 is $-\begin{vmatrix} 2 & 3 & 4 \\ 1 & 6 & 0 \\ 0 & -5 & 0 \end{vmatrix} = 20.$

Exercise 5.3

2 Facoring out the k in each successive column (or row)--for a total of n columns (or rows)--will yield the indicated result.

3 (a) Property IV. (b) Property III (applied to both rows).

4 (a) Nonsingular. (b) Singular. (c) Singular. (d) Nonsingular.

5 In (a) and (d), the rank is 3. In (b) and (c), the rank is less than 3 (equal to 2).

6 No, because each set is linearly dependent--when the three vectors are combined into a matrix, its determinant vanishes.

7 A is nonsingular because $|A| = 1 - b \neq 0$.

Exercise 5.4

1 They are $\sum_{i=1}^{4} a_{i3}|C_{i2}|$ and $\sum_{j=1}^{4} a_{2j}|C_{4j}|$, respectively.

2 Since adj A = $\begin{bmatrix} 1 & -2 \\ 0 & 5 \end{bmatrix}$, We have $A^{-1} = \frac{\text{adj } A}{|A|} = \frac{1}{5}\begin{bmatrix} 1 & -2 \\ 0 & 5 \end{bmatrix}$.

Similarly, we have $B^{-1} = \frac{1}{2}\begin{bmatrix} 2 & 0 \\ -9 & 1 \end{bmatrix}$, $C^{-1} = \frac{-1}{28}\begin{bmatrix} -1 & -7 \\ -3 & 7 \end{bmatrix}$,

and $D^{-1} = \frac{1}{21}\begin{bmatrix} 3 & -6 \\ 0 & 7 \end{bmatrix}$.

3 (a) Interchange the two diagonal elements of A; multiply the two off-diagonal elements of A by -1.

(b) Divide the adj A by $|A|$.

4 $E^{-1} = \frac{1}{8}\begin{bmatrix} 3 & 2 & -9 \\ -1 & 2 & -5 \\ -6 & -4 & 26 \end{bmatrix}$, $F^{-1} = \frac{-1}{10}\begin{bmatrix} 0 & 2 & -3 \\ 10 & -6 & -1 \\ 0 & -4 & 1 \end{bmatrix}$,

$G^{-1} = \begin{bmatrix} 1 & 0 & 0 \\ 0 & 0 & 1 \\ 0 & 1 & 0 \end{bmatrix}$, $H^{-1} = \begin{bmatrix} 1 & 0 & 0 \\ 0 & 1 & 0 \\ 0 & 0 & 1 \end{bmatrix}$.

5 Yes, matrices G and H in the preceding problem are examples.

Exercise 5.5

1 (a) $|A| = 7$, $|A_1| = 35$, $|A_2| = 14$. Thus $\bar{x}_1 = 5$, $\bar{x}_2 = 2$.

(b) $|A| = -11$, $|A_1| = -33$, $|A_2| = 0$. Thus $\bar{x}_1 = 3$, $\bar{x}_2 = 0$.

(c) $|A| = 15$, $|A_1| = 15$, $|A_2| = 30$. Thus $\bar{x}_1 = 1$, $\bar{x}_2 = 2$.

(d) $|A| = |A_1| = |A_2| = -81$. Thus $\bar{x}_1 = \bar{x}_2 = 1$.

2 (a) $A^{-1} = \frac{1}{7}\begin{bmatrix} 1 & 2 \\ -2 & 3 \end{bmatrix}$, and $\bar{x} = A^{-1}d = \begin{bmatrix} 5 \\ 2 \end{bmatrix}$.

(b) $A^{-1} = \frac{-1}{11}\begin{bmatrix} -1 & -3 \\ -4 & -1 \end{bmatrix}$, and $\bar{x} = A^{-1}d = \begin{bmatrix} 3 \\ 0 \end{bmatrix}$.

(c) $A^{-1} = \frac{1}{15}\begin{bmatrix} 1 & 7 \\ -1 & 8 \end{bmatrix}$, and $\bar{x} = A^{-1}d = \begin{bmatrix} 1 \\ 2 \end{bmatrix}$.

(d) $A^{-1} = \frac{-1}{81}\begin{bmatrix} -3 & -9 \\ -7 & 6 \end{bmatrix}$, and $\bar{x} = A^{-1}d = \begin{bmatrix} 1 \\ 1 \end{bmatrix}$.

3 (a) $|A| = 14$, $|A_1| = 28$, $|A_2| = 14$, $|A_3| = 0$; thus $\bar{x}_1 = 2$, $\bar{x}_2 = 1$, $\bar{x}_3 = 0$.

(b) $|A| = 18$, $|A_1| = -18$, $|A_2| = 54$, $|A_3| = 126$;
thus $\bar{x}_1 = -1$, $\bar{x}_2 = 3$, $\bar{x}_3 = 7$.

(c) $|A| = 10$, $|A_1| = 0$, $|A_2| = 50$, $|A_3| = 40$;
thus $\bar{x} = 0$, $\bar{y} = 5$, $\bar{z} = 4$.

(d) $|A| = 4$, $|A_1| = 2(b + c)$, $|A_2| = 2(a + c)$, $|A_3| = 2(a + b)$;
thus $\bar{x} = \frac{1}{2}(b + c)$, $\bar{y} = \frac{1}{2}(a + c)$, $\bar{z} = \frac{1}{2}(a + b)$.

After the indicated multiplication by the appropriate cofactors, the new equations will add up to the following equation:

$$\sum_{i=1}^{n} a_{i1}|C_{ij}|x_1 + \sum_{i=1}^{n} a_{i2}|C_{ij}|x_2 + \cdots + \sum_{i=1}^{n} a_{in}|C_{ij}|x_n = \sum_{i=1}^{n} d_i|C_{ij}|$$

When $j = 1$, the coefficient of x_1 becomes $|A|$, whereas the coefficients of the other variables all vanish; thus the last equation reduces to $|A|x_1 = \sum_{i=1}^{n} d_i|C_{i1}|$, leading to the result for $\bar{x}_1$ in (5.14). When $j = 2$, we similarly get the result for $\bar{x}_2$.

Exercise 5.6

1 The system can be written as $\begin{bmatrix} 1 & -1 & 0 \\ -b & 1 & b \\ -t & 0 & 1 \end{bmatrix}\begin{bmatrix} Y \\ C \\ T \end{bmatrix} = \begin{bmatrix} I_0 + G_0 \\ a \\ d \end{bmatrix}$

(a) Since $A^{-1} = \frac{1}{1 - b + bt}\begin{bmatrix} 1 & 1 & -b \\ b(1-t) & 1 & -b \\ t & t & 1-b \end{bmatrix}$, the solution is

$$\begin{bmatrix} \bar{Y} \\ \bar{C} \\ \bar{T} \end{bmatrix} = A^{-1}d = \frac{1}{1 - b + bt}\begin{bmatrix} I_0 + G_0 + a - bd \\ b(1 - t)(I_0 + G_0) + a - bd \\ t(I_0 + G_0) + at + d(1 - b) \end{bmatrix}$$

(b) $|A| = 1 - b + bt$ $\quad\quad |A_1| = I_0 + G_0 - bd + a$

$|A_2| = a - bd + b(1 - t)(I_0 + G_0)$

$|A_3| = d(1 - b) + t(a + I_0 + G_0)$

Thus $\overline{Y} = \dfrac{I_0 + G_0 - bd + a}{1 - b + bt}$ $\quad\quad \overline{C} = \dfrac{a - bd + b(1 - t)(I_0 + G_0)}{1 - b + bt}$

and $\overline{T} = \dfrac{d(1 - b) + t(a + I_0 + G_0)}{1 - b + bt}$

2 The system is $\begin{bmatrix} 1 & -1 & -1 \\ -b & 1 & 0 \\ -g & 0 & 1 \end{bmatrix} \begin{bmatrix} Y \\ C \\ G \end{bmatrix} = \begin{bmatrix} I_0 \\ a - bT_0 \\ 0 \end{bmatrix}$

(a) Since $A^{-1} = \dfrac{1}{1 - b - g} \begin{bmatrix} 1 & 1 & 1 \\ b & 1-g & b \\ g & g & 1-b \end{bmatrix}$, the solution is

$$\begin{bmatrix} \overline{Y} \\ \overline{C} \\ \overline{G} \end{bmatrix} = A^{-1}d = \frac{1}{1 - b - g} \begin{bmatrix} I_0 + a - bT_0 \\ bI_0 + (1 - g)(a - bT_0) \\ g(I_0 + a - bT_0) \end{bmatrix}$$

(b) $|A| = 1 - b - g$ $\quad\quad |A_1| = I_0 + a - bT_0$

$|A_2| = (1 - g)(a - bT_0) + bI_0$

$|A_3| = g(a - bT_0 + I_0)$

Thus $\overline{Y} = \dfrac{I_0 + a - bT_0}{1 - b - g}$ $\quad\quad \overline{C} = \dfrac{(1 - g)(a - bT_0) + bI_0}{1 - b - g}$

and $\overline{G} = \dfrac{g(a - bT_0 + I_0)}{1 - b - g}$

Exercise 5.7

1 $\begin{bmatrix} \overline{x}_1 \\ \overline{x}_2 \\ \overline{x}_3 \end{bmatrix} = \dfrac{1}{0.384} \begin{bmatrix} 0.66 & 0.30 & 0.24 \\ 0.34 & 0.62 & 0.24 \\ 0.21 & 0.27 & 0.60 \end{bmatrix} \begin{bmatrix} 30 \\ 15 \\ 10 \end{bmatrix} = \dfrac{1}{0.384} \begin{bmatrix} 26.70 \\ 21.90 \\ 16.35 \end{bmatrix} = \begin{bmatrix} 69.53 \\ 57.03 \\ 42.58 \end{bmatrix}$

2 $\sum_{j=1}^{3} a_{0j}\overline{x}_j = 0.3(69.53) + 0.3(57.03) + 0.4(42.58) =$ \$55.00 billion

3 (a) $A = \begin{bmatrix} 0.10 & 0.50 \\ 0.60 & 0 \end{bmatrix}$, $T = \begin{bmatrix} 0.90 & -0.50 \\ -0.60 & 1.00 \end{bmatrix}$. Thus the matrix

equation is $\begin{bmatrix} 0.90 & -0.50 \\ -0.60 & 1.00 \end{bmatrix} \begin{bmatrix} x_1 \\ x_2 \end{bmatrix} = \begin{bmatrix} 1000 \\ 2000 \end{bmatrix}$.

(b) $|A| = 0.60$, $|A_1| = 2000$, $|A_2| = 2400$. Thus $\bar{x}_1 = 3333\frac{1}{3}$, and $\bar{x}_2 = 4000$.

4 (a) Element 0.33: 33¢ of commodity II is needed as input for producing $1 of commodity I.

Element 0: Industry III does not use its own output as its input.

Element 200: The open sector demands 200 (billion dollars) of commodity II.

(b) Third-column sum = 0.46, meaning that 46¢ of non-primary inputs are used in producing $1 of commodity III.

(c) No significant economic meaning.

(d) $\begin{bmatrix} 0.95 & -0.25 & -0.34 \\ -0.33 & 0.90 & -0.12 \\ -0.19 & -0.38 & 1.00 \end{bmatrix} \begin{bmatrix} x_1 \\ x_2 \\ x_3 \end{bmatrix} = \begin{bmatrix} 1800 \\ 200 \\ 900 \end{bmatrix}$

5 From part (d) of the preceding problem, we find that

$|A| = 0.62$ (rounded from 0.6227), $|A_1| = 1916.16$, $|A_2| = 1015.70$, and $|A_3| = 1310.47$. Thus we have, approximately:

$\bar{x}_1 = 3090.58$ $\quad \bar{x}_2 = 1638.23$ $\quad \bar{x}_3 = 2113.66$

CHAPTER 6

Exercise 6.2

1 (a) $\frac{\Delta y}{\Delta x} = \frac{4(x + \Delta x)^2 + 9 - (4x^2 + 9)}{\Delta x} = 8x + 4\Delta x$

(b) $dy/dx = f'(x) = 8x$ (c) $f'(3) = 24$ and $f'(4) = 32$

2 (a) $\Delta y/\Delta x = 10x + 5\Delta x - 4$ (b) $dy/dx = 10x - 4$

(c) $f'(2) = 16$ and $f'(3) = 26$

3 (a) $\Delta y/\Delta x = 5$; a constant function. (b) No; $dy/dx = 5$.

Exercise 6.4

1 Left-side limit = right-side limit = 15. Yes, the limit is 15.

2 The function can be rewritten as $q = (v^3 + 4v^2 + 8v)/v = v^2 + 4v + 8$, $(v \neq 0)$. Thus:

(a) $\lim_{v \to 0} q = 8$ (b) $\lim_{v \to 2} q = 20$ (c) $\lim_{v \to a} q = a^2 + 4a + 8$

3 (a) 5 (b) 5

4 If we choose a very small neighborhood of the point $L + a_2$, we cannot find a neighborhood of N such that for every value of v in the N-neighborhood, q will be in the $(L + a_2)$-neighborhood.

Exercise 6.5

1 (a) Adding $-3x - 2$ to both sides, we get $-3 < 4x$. Multiplying both sides of the latter by 1/4, we get the solution $-3/4 < x$.

(b) The solution is $x < -9$. (c) The solution is $x < 1/2$.

(d) The solution is $-3/2 < x$.

2 The continued inequality is $7x - 3 < 0 < 7x$. Adding $-7x$ to all sides, and then multiplying by $-1/7$ (thereby reversing the sense of inequality), we get the solution $0 < x < 3/7$.

3 (a) By (6.9), we can write $-6 < x + 1 < 6$. Subtracting 1 from all sides, we get $-7 < x < 5$ as the solution.

(b) The solution is $2/3 < x < 2$. (c) The solution is $-4 \le x \le 1$.

Exercise 6.6

1 (a) $\lim_{v \to 0} q = 8 - 0 + 0 = 8$ (b) $\lim_{v \to 3} q = 8 - 27 + 9 = -10$

(c) $\lim_{v \to -1} q = 8 + 9 + 1 = 18$

(a) $\lim_{v \to -1} q = \lim_{v \to -1} (v + 2) \cdot \lim_{v \to -1} (v - 3) = 1(-4) = -4$

(b) $\lim_{v \to 0} q = 2(-3) = -6$ (c) $\lim_{v \to 4} q = 6(1) = 6$

; (a) $\lim_{v \to 0} q = \lim_{v \to 0} (3v + 5)/\lim_{v \to 0} (v + 2) = 5/2 = 2\frac{1}{2}$

(b) $\lim_{v \to 5} q = (15 + 5)/(5 + 2) = 20/7 = 2\frac{6}{7}$

(c) $\lim_{v \to -1} q = (-3 + 5)/(-1 + 2) = 2/1 = 2$

Exercise 6.7

1

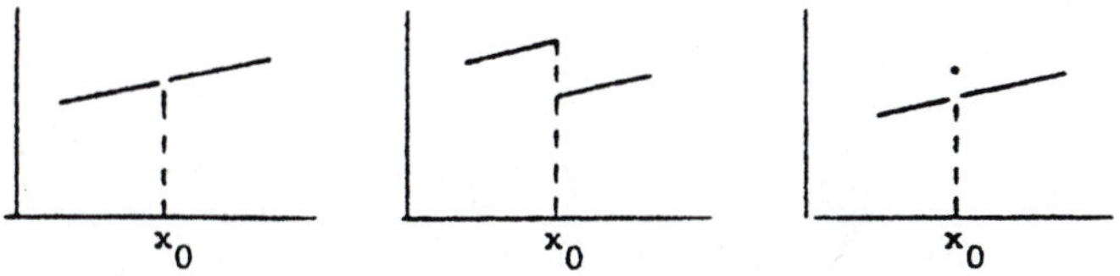

2 (a) $\lim_{v \to N} q = N^2 - 7N - 3 = g(N)$ (b) Yes. (c) Yes.

3 (a) $\lim_{v \to N} q = (N + 2)/(N^2 + 2) = g(N)$

(b) Yes. (c) The function is continuous in the domain.

4 (a) No. (b) No, because $f(x)$ is not defined at $x = 4$; i.e., $x = 4$ is not in the domain of the function.

(c) For $x \neq 4$, the function reduces to $y = x + 5$, so $\lim_{x \to 4} y = 9$.

5 No, because $q = v + 1$, as such, is defined at every value of v, whereas the given rational function is <u>not</u> defined at $v = 2$ and

$v = -2$. The only permissible way to rewrite is to qualify the equation $q = v + 1$ by the restrictions $v \neq 2$ and $v \neq -2$.

6 Yes; each function is not only continuous but also smooth.

CHAPTER 7

Exercise 7.1

(a) $dy/dx = 13x^{12}$ (b) $dy/dx = 0$ (c) $dy/dx = 42x^5$

(d) $dw/du = -3u^{-2}$ (e) $dw/du = -2u^{-1/2}$

(a) $4x^{-5}$ (b) $\frac{7}{3}x^{-2/3}$ (c) $36w^3$ (d) $2cx$ (e) abu^{b-1}

(a) $f'(x) = 18$; thus $f'(1) = f'(2) = 18$.

(b) $f'(x) = 3cx^2$; thus $f'(1) = 3c$ and $f'(2) = 12c$.

(c) $f'(x) = 10x^{-3}$; thus $f'(1) = 10$ and $f'(2) = \frac{10}{8} = 1\frac{1}{4}$.

(d) $f'(x) = x^{1/3} = \sqrt[3]{x}$; thus $f'(1) = 1$ and $f'(2) = \sqrt[3]{2}$.

(e) $f'(w) = 2w^{-2/3}$; thus $f'(1) = 2$ and $f'(2) = 2 \cdot 2^{-2/3} = 2^{1/3}$.

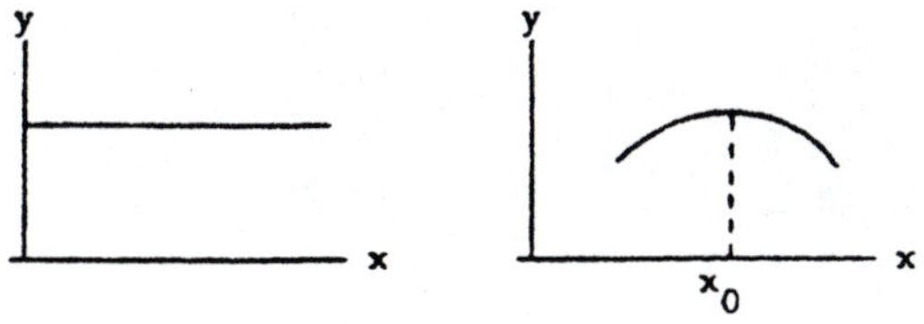

Exercise 7.2

1 $VC = Q^3 - 5Q^2 + 14Q$. The derivative $\frac{d}{dQ}VC = 3Q^2 - 10Q + 14$ is the MC function.

2 $C = AC \cdot Q = Q^3 - 4Q^2 + 214Q$. Thus $MC = dC/dQ = 3Q^2 - 8Q + 214$. Since the total-cost funciton shows a zero fixed cost, the situation depicted is the long run.

3 (a) $3(27x^2 + 6x - 2)$ (b) $54x^2 + 102x - 55$

(c) $12x(x + 1)$ (d) $cx(3ax - 2b)$

(e) $-x(9x + 14)$ (f) $2 - \frac{x^2 + 3}{x^2} = \frac{x^2 - 3}{x^2}$

4 (b) $R = AR \cdot Q = 60Q - 3Q^2$, and $MR = dR/dQ = 60 - 6Q$.

(c) It should.

(d) The MR curve is twice as steep as the AR curve.

5 Let the average curve be represented by $A = a + bx$. Then the total curve will be $T = A \cdot x = ax + bx^2$, and the marginal curve will be $M = dT/dx = a + 2bx$.

6 Let $\phi(x) \equiv g(x)h(x)$; this implies that $\phi'(x) = g'(x)h(x) + g(x)h'(x)$. Then we may write

$$\frac{d}{dx}[f(x)g(x)h(x)] = \frac{d}{dx}[f(x)\phi(x)] = f'(x)\phi(x) + f(x)\phi'(x)$$

$$= f'(x)g(x)h(x) + f(x)[g'(x)h(x) + g(x)h'(x)]$$

$$= f'(x)g(x)h(x) + f(x)g'(x)h(x) + f(x)g(x)h'(x)$$

7 (a) $\dfrac{x^2 - 3}{x^2}$ (b) $-\dfrac{7}{x^2}$ (c) $\dfrac{20}{(x + 5)^2}$ (d) $\dfrac{acx^2 + 2adx - bc}{(cx + d)^2}$

8 (a) $\dfrac{d}{dx}(ax + b) = a$ (b) $\dfrac{d}{dx}\,x(ax + b) = 2ax + b$

(c) $\dfrac{d}{dx}\dfrac{1}{ax + b} = \dfrac{-a}{(ax + b)^2}$ (d) $\dfrac{d}{dx}\dfrac{ax + b}{x} = \dfrac{-b}{x^2}$

Exercise 7.3

1 $dy/dx = (dy/du)(du/dx) = 3u^2(-2x) = -6x(5 - x^2)^2$

2 $dw/dx = (dw/dy)(dy/dx) = 2ay(2bx + c) = 2ax(2b^2x^2 + 3bcx + c^2)$

3 (a) Let $w = 3x^2 - 13$; this implies that $dw/dx = 6x$. Since $y = w^3$, we have $\dfrac{dy}{dx} = \dfrac{dy}{dw}\dfrac{dw}{dx} = 3w^2(6x) = 18x(3x^2 - 13)^2$.

(b) $\dfrac{dy}{dx} = 216x^2(8x^3 - 5)^8$ (c) $\dfrac{dy}{dx} = 4a(ax + b)^3$

4 Both methods yield the same answer $dy/dx = -32(16x + 3)^{-3}$.

5 The inverse function is $x = \dfrac{y}{7} - 3$. The derivatives are $dy/dx = 7$ and $dx/dy = 1/7$; thus the inverse-function rule is verified.

6 (a) Since $x > 0$, we have $dy/dx = -6x^5 < 0$ for all admissible values of x. Thus the function is monotonically decreasing, and dx/dy is equal to $-1/6x^5$, the reciprocal of dy/dx.

(b) $dy/dx = 20x^4 + 3x^2 + 3 > 0$ for any value of x; thus the function is monotonically increasing, and $dx/dy = 1/(20x^4 + 3x^2 + 3)$.

Exercise 7.4

1 (a) $\partial y/\partial x_1 = 6x_1^2 - 22x_1x_2$ $\quad \partial y/\partial x_2 = -11x_1^2 + 6x_2$

(b) $\partial y/\partial x_1 = 7 + 5x_2^2$ $\quad \partial y/\partial x_2 = 10x_1x_2 - 27x_2^2$

(c) $\partial y/\partial x_1 = 2(x_2 - 2)$ $\quad \partial y/\partial x_2 = 2x_1 + 3$

(d) $\partial y/\partial x_1 = 4/(x_2 - 2)$ $\quad \partial y/\partial x_2 = -(4x_1 + 3)/(x_2 - 2)^2$

2 (a) $f_x = 2x + 5y$ $\quad f_y = 5x - 3y^2$

(b) $f_x = 3x^2 - 4x - 3y$ $\quad f_y = -3(x - 2)$

(c) $f_x = 5y/(x + y)^2$ $\quad f_y = -5x/(x + y)^2$

(d) $f_x = (x^2 + 1)/x^2y$ $\quad f_y = -(x^2 - 1)/xy^2$

3 (a) 12 (b) -7 (c) 10/9 (d) 1

4 $MPP_K = (0.3)96K^{-0.7}L^{0.7}$ $\quad MPP_L = (0.7)96K^{0.3}L^{-0.3}$

5 (a) $U_1 = 2(x_1 + 2)(x_2 + 3)^3$ $\quad U_2 = 3(x_1 + 2)^2(x_2 + 3)^2$

(b) $U_1(3,3) = 2160$

Exercise 7.5

1 $\frac{\partial\overline{Q}}{\partial a} = \frac{d}{b + d} > 0$ $\quad \frac{\partial\overline{Q}}{\partial b} = \frac{-d(a + c)}{(b + d)^2} < 0$

$\frac{\partial\overline{Q}}{\partial c} = \frac{-b}{b + d} < 0$ $\quad \frac{\partial\overline{Q}}{\partial d} = \frac{b(a + c)}{(b + d)^2} > 0$

2 $\frac{\partial\overline{Y}}{\partial I_0}$ (investment multiplier) $= \frac{\partial\overline{Y}}{\partial\alpha}$ (consumption multiplier)

$$= \frac{1}{1 - \beta + \beta\delta} > 0$$

$\frac{\partial\overline{Y}}{\partial\beta}$ (MPC multiplier) $= \dfrac{-\gamma + (1 - \delta)(\alpha + I_0 + G_0)}{(1 - \beta + \beta\delta)^2}$

$$= \frac{-\gamma + (1 - \delta)\overline{Y}}{(1 - \beta + \beta\delta)} \text{ [by (7.18)]}$$

$$= \frac{\overline{Y} - \overline{T}}{(1 - \beta + \beta\delta)} \text{ [by (7.17)].}$$

Assuming non-confiscatory taxation, we can take $\frac{\partial\overline{Y}}{\partial\beta}$ to be positive.

3 (a) Nine.

(b) $\dfrac{\partial \bar{x}_1}{\partial d_1} = \dfrac{0.66}{0.384}$ $\qquad \dfrac{\partial \bar{x}_1}{\partial d_2} = \dfrac{0.30}{0.384}$ $\qquad \dfrac{\partial \bar{x}_1}{\partial d_3} = \dfrac{0.24}{0.384}$

$\dfrac{\partial \bar{x}_2}{\partial d_1} = \dfrac{0.34}{0.384}$ $\qquad \dfrac{\partial \bar{x}_2}{\partial d_2} = \dfrac{0.62}{0.384}$ $\qquad \dfrac{\partial \bar{x}_2}{\partial d_3} = \dfrac{0.24}{0.384}$

$\dfrac{\partial \bar{x}_3}{\partial d_1} = \dfrac{0.21}{0.384}$ $\qquad \dfrac{\partial \bar{x}_3}{\partial d_2} = \dfrac{0.27}{0.384}$ $\qquad \dfrac{\partial \bar{x}_3}{\partial d_3} = \dfrac{0.60}{0.384}$

or $\dfrac{\partial \bar{x}}{\partial d_1} = \dfrac{1}{0.384}\begin{bmatrix}0.66\\0.34\\0.21\end{bmatrix}$, $\dfrac{\partial \bar{x}}{\partial d_2} = \dfrac{1}{0.384}\begin{bmatrix}0.30\\0.62\\0.27\end{bmatrix}$, $\dfrac{\partial \bar{x}}{\partial d_3} = \dfrac{1}{0.384}\begin{bmatrix}0.24\\0.24\\0.60\end{bmatrix}$

Exercise 7.6

1 (a) $|J| = \begin{vmatrix} 6x_1 & 1 \\ (36x_1^3 + 12x_1x_2 + 48x_1) & (6x_1^2 + 2x_2 + 8) \end{vmatrix} = 0$

The functions are dependent.

(b) $|J| = \begin{vmatrix} 6x_1 & 4x_2 \\ 5 & 0 \end{vmatrix} = -20x_2$

Since $|J|$ is not identically zero, the functions are independent.

2 (a) $|J| = \begin{vmatrix} b_{11} & b_{12} & b_{13} \\ b_{21} & b_{22} & b_{23} \\ b_{31} & b_{32} & b_{33} \end{vmatrix} = |B|$

(b) Since B has an inverse matrix (I - A), it must be nonsingular, and so $|B| \neq 0$, or $|J| \neq 0$. The equations in (7.22) are thus functionally independent.

CHAPTER 8

Exercise 8.1

1 (a) $dy = -3(x^2 + 1)\,dx$ (b) $dy = (14x - 51)\,dx$

(c) $$dy = \frac{1 - x^2}{(x^2 + 1)^2}\,dx$$

$$\varepsilon_{MY} = \frac{dM/dY}{M/Y} = \frac{\text{marginal propensity to import}}{\text{average propensity to import}}$$

(a) $dC/dY = b$ $C/Y = (a + bY)/Y$

(b) $$\varepsilon_{CY} = \frac{dC/dY}{C/Y} = \frac{bY}{a + bY} > 0$$

(c) Since $bY < a + bY$, it follows that $\varepsilon_{CY} < 1$.

Since $Q = kP^{-n}$, with $dQ/dP = -nkP^{-n-1}$ and $Q/P = kP^{-n-1}$, the point elasticity is $\varepsilon_d = -n =$ a constant. (a) No. (b) When $n = 1$, the demand function is $Q = k/P$, which plots as a rectangular hyperbola, with a unitary point elasticity everywhere.

Exercise 8.2

1 (a) $dz = (6x + y)\,dx + (x - 6y^2)\,dy$

(b) $dU = (2 + 9x_2)\,dx_1 + (9x_1 + 2x_2)\,dx_2$

2 (a) $$dy = \frac{x_2}{(x_1 + x_2)^2}\,dx_1 - \frac{x_1}{(x_1 + x_2)^2}\,dx_2$$

(b) $$dy = 2\left(\frac{x_2}{x_1 + x_2}\right)^2 dx_1 + 2\left(\frac{x_1}{x_1 + x_2}\right)^2 dx_2$$

3 $$\frac{\partial Q}{\partial P} = 2bP, \text{ thus } \varepsilon_{QP} = 2bP\frac{P}{Q} = \frac{2bP^2}{(a + bP^2 + R^{1/2})};$$

$$\frac{\partial Q}{\partial R} = \frac{1}{2}R^{-1/2}, \text{ thus } \varepsilon_{QR} = \frac{1}{2}R^{-1/2}\frac{R}{Q} = \frac{R^{1/2}}{2(a + bP^2 + R^{1/2})}.$$

4 $$\frac{\partial}{\partial P}\varepsilon_{QP} = \frac{4bP(a + R^{1/2})}{(a + bP^2 + R^{1/2})^2} \gtreqless 0 \text{ as } (a + R^{1/2}) \gtreqless 0$$

$$\frac{\partial}{\partial R}\epsilon_{QP} = \frac{-bP^2R^{-1/2}}{(a + bP^2 + R^{1/2})^2} < 0$$

$$\frac{\partial}{\partial P}\epsilon_{QR} = \frac{-bPR^{1/2}}{(a + bP^2 + R^{1/2})^2} < 0$$

$$\frac{\partial}{\partial R}\epsilon_{QR} = \frac{R^{-1/2}(a + bP^2)}{4(a + bP^2 + R^{1/2})^2} \gtreqless 0 \text{ as } (a + bP^2) \gtreqless 0$$

Each of these derivatives adheres to a single sign, thus each elasticity varies with P and R in a monotonic fashion. (Note that even $\frac{\partial}{\partial P}\epsilon_{QP}$ adheres to a single sign, because in the context of that derivative, R is a constant, so that $(a + R^{1/2})$ has a single magnitude with a single sign. The same reasoning applies also to $\frac{\partial}{\partial R}\epsilon_{QR}$.)

5 $\epsilon_{XP} = \frac{\partial X/\partial P}{X/P} = \frac{-2P^{-3}}{Y_f^{1/2}P^{-1} + P^{-3}} = \frac{-2}{Y_f^{1/2}P^2 + 1}$

Exercise 8.3

1 (a) $dz = 6x\,dx + (y\,dx + x\,dy) - 6y^2\,dy = (6x + y)dx + (x - 6y^2)dy$

(b) $dU = 2dx_1 + (9x_2\,dx_1 + 9x_1\,dx_2) + 2x_2\,dx_2$

$= (2 + 9x_2)dx_1 + (9x_1 + 2x_2)dx_2$

2 (a) $dy = \frac{(x_1 + x_2)dx_1 - x_1(dx_1 + dx_2)}{(x_1 + x_2)^2} = \frac{x_2\,dx_1 - x_1\,dx_2}{(x_1 + x_2)^2}$

(b) $dy = \frac{(x_1 + x_2)(2x_2\,dx_1 + 2x_1\,dx_2) - 2x_1x_2(dx_1 + dx_2)}{(x_1 + x_2)^2}$

$= \frac{2x_2^2\,dx_1 + 2x_1^2\,dx_2}{(x_1 + x_2)^2}$

3 (a) $dy = 3[(2x_2 - 1)(x_3 + 5)dx_1 + 2x_1(x_3 + 5)dx_2 + x_1(2x_2 - 1)dx_3]$

(b) $dy = 3(2x_2 - 1)(x_3 + 5)dx_1$ (c) $\frac{\partial y}{\partial x_1} = 3(2x_2 - 1)(x_3 + 5)$

4 Rule II: $d(cu^n) = (\frac{d}{du} cu^n)\, du = cnu^{n-1}\, du$

Rule III: $d(u \pm v) = \frac{\partial(u \pm v)}{\partial u} du + \frac{\partial(u \pm v)}{\partial v} dv = 1du + (\pm 1)dv$

$= du \pm dv$

Rule IV: $d(uv) = \frac{\partial(uv)}{\partial u} du + \frac{\partial(uv)}{\partial v} dv = v\, du + u\, dv$

Rule V: $d(\frac{u}{v}) = \frac{\partial(u/v)}{\partial u} du + \frac{\partial(u/v)}{\partial v} dv = \frac{1}{v} du - \frac{u}{v^2} dv$

$= \frac{1}{v^2}(v\, du - u\, dv)$

Exercise 8.4

1 (a) $\frac{dz}{dy} = \frac{\partial z}{\partial y} + \frac{\partial z}{\partial x}\frac{dx}{dy} = x - 2y + (2 + y)(6y) = x + 10y + 6y^2$

$= 10y + 9y^2$

(b) $dz/dy = 4y - 12/y^3$ (c) $dz/dy = -15x + 3y = 108y - 30$

2 (a) $\frac{dz}{dt} = \frac{\partial z}{\partial x}\frac{dx}{dt} + \frac{\partial z}{\partial y}\frac{dy}{dt} = (2x - 8y)(3) + (-8x - 3y^2)(-1)$

$= 14x - 24y + 3y^2 = 3t^2 + 60t - 21$

(b) $dz/dt = 3(4t) + t(1) + v = 13t + v = 14t + 1$

(c) $dz/dt = bf_x + df_y + f_t$

3 $\frac{dQ}{dt} = a\alpha AK^{\alpha-1}L^{\beta} + b\beta AK^{\alpha}L^{\beta-1} + A'(t)K^{\alpha}L^{\beta}$

$= [a\alpha A/K + b\beta A/L + A'(t)]K^{\alpha}L^{\beta}$

4 (a) $\frac{\S W}{\S u} = \frac{\partial W}{\partial x}\frac{\partial x}{\partial u} + \frac{\partial W}{\partial y}\frac{\partial y}{\partial u} + \frac{\partial W}{\partial u} = (2ax + by)(\alpha) + (bx)(\gamma) + c$

$= \alpha[2a(\alpha u + \beta v) + b\gamma u] + b\gamma(\alpha u + \beta v) + c$

$\frac{\S W}{\S v} = \frac{\partial W}{\partial x}\frac{\partial x}{\partial v} + \frac{\partial W}{\partial y}\frac{\partial y}{\partial v} = (2ax + by)\,(\beta) + (bx)\,(0)$

$= \beta[2a(\alpha u + \beta v) + b\gamma u]$

(b) $\frac{\S W}{\S u} = 10uf_1 + f_2$ $\frac{\S W}{\S v} = 3f_1 - 12v^2 f_2$

5

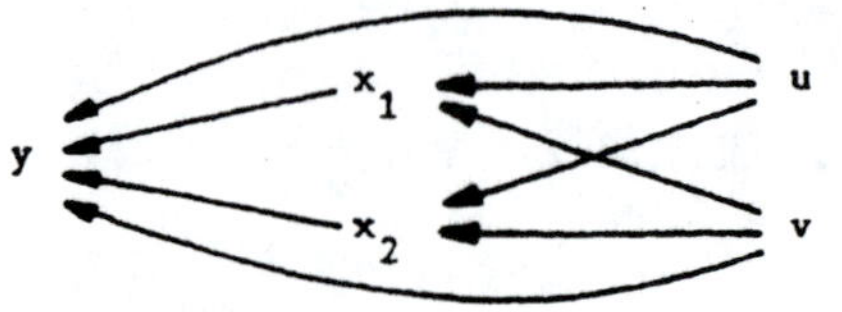

6 $\frac{\S y}{\S v} = \frac{\partial y}{\partial x_1}\frac{\partial x_1}{\partial v} + \frac{\partial y}{\partial x_2}\frac{\partial x_2}{\partial v} + \frac{\partial y}{\partial v}$

Exercise 8.5

1 (a) $\frac{\partial U}{\partial x_2} = -\frac{\partial F/\partial x_2}{\partial F/\partial U}$, $\frac{\partial U}{\partial x_n} = -\frac{\partial F/\partial x_n}{\partial F/\partial U}$, $\frac{\partial x_3}{\partial x_2} = -\frac{\partial F/\partial x_2}{\partial F/\partial x_3}$, $\frac{\partial x_4}{\partial x_n} = -\frac{\partial F/\partial x_n}{\partial F/\partial x_4}$

(b) The first two are marginal utilities; the last two are slopes of indifference curves (negatives of marginal rates of substitution).

2 (a) Point (y=3, x=1) does satisfy the given equation. Moreover, $F_x = 3x^2 - 4xy + 3y^2$ and $F_y = -2x^2 + 6xy$ are continuous, and $F_y = 16 \neq 0$ at the given point. Thus an implicit function is defined, with:

$$\frac{dy}{dx} = -\frac{F_x}{F_y} = -\frac{3x^2 - 4xy + 3y^2}{-2x^2 + 6xy} = -\frac{18}{16} = -\frac{9}{8} \text{ at the given point}$$

(b) The given point satisfies this equation also. Since both $F_x = 4x + 4y$ and $F_y = 4x - 4y^3$ are continuous, and $F_y = -104 \neq 0$ at the given point, an implicit function is again defined.

$$\frac{dy}{dx} = -\frac{4x + 4y}{4x - 4y^3} = -\frac{16}{-104} = \frac{2}{13} \text{ at the given point}$$

3 Point (x=1, y=2, z=0) satisfies the given equation. Since the three derivatives $F_x = 2x + 3y$, $F_y = 3x + 2z + 2y$, $F_z = 2y + 2z$ are all continuous, and $F_z = 4 \neq 0$ at the given point, an implicit function $z = f(x, y)$ is defined. At the given point, we have

$$\frac{\partial z}{\partial x} = -\frac{2x + 3y}{2y + 2z} = -2 \qquad \frac{\partial z}{\partial y} = -\frac{3x + 2z + 2y}{2y + 2z} = -\frac{7}{4}$$

4 The given equation can be solved for y, to yield the function y = x

(with the 45° line as its graph). Yet, at the point (0, 0), which satisfies the given equation and is on the 45° line, we find $F_y = -3(x-y)^2 = 0$, which violates the condition of a nonzero F_y as cited in the theorem. This serves to show that this condition is not a necessary condition for the function $y = f(x)$ to be defined.

By (8.19), $\frac{\partial z}{\partial x}\frac{\partial x}{\partial y}\frac{\partial y}{\partial z} = \left(-\frac{F_x}{F_z}\right)\left(-\frac{F_y}{F_x}\right)\left(-\frac{F_z}{F_y}\right) = -1.$

At least one of the partial derivatives in the vector of constants in (8.23') must be nonzero; otherwise, the variable x_1 does not affect F^1, F^2 and F^3, and has no legitimate status as an argument in the F functions in (8.20).

To find the nonincome-tax multiplier $\partial\overline{Y}/\partial\gamma$ (along with $\partial\overline{C}/\partial\gamma$ and $\partial\overline{T}/\partial\gamma$), the relevant matrix equation is

$$\begin{bmatrix} 1 & -1 & 0 \\ -\beta & 1 & \beta \\ -\delta & 0 & 1 \end{bmatrix}\begin{bmatrix} \partial\overline{Y}/\partial\gamma \\ \partial\overline{C}/\partial\gamma \\ \partial\overline{T}/\partial\gamma \end{bmatrix} = \begin{bmatrix} -\partial F^1/\partial\gamma \\ -\partial F^2/\partial\gamma \\ -\partial F^3/\partial\gamma \end{bmatrix} = \begin{bmatrix} 0 \\ 0 \\ 1 \end{bmatrix}$$

$$\text{Thus } \frac{\partial\overline{Y}}{\partial\gamma} = \frac{\begin{vmatrix} 0 & -1 & 0 \\ 0 & 1 & \beta \\ 1 & 0 & 1 \end{vmatrix}}{|J|} = \frac{-\beta}{1-\beta+\beta\delta} \qquad \text{[by (8.26)]}$$

To find the income-tax-rate multiplier $\partial\overline{Y}/\partial\delta$ (along with $\partial\overline{C}/\partial\delta$ and $\partial\overline{T}/\partial\delta$), the relevant matrix equation is

$$\begin{bmatrix} 1 & -1 & 0 \\ -\beta & 1 & \beta \\ -\delta & 0 & 1 \end{bmatrix}\begin{bmatrix} \partial\overline{Y}/\partial\delta \\ \partial\overline{C}/\partial\delta \\ \partial\overline{T}/\partial\delta \end{bmatrix} = \begin{bmatrix} -\partial F^1/\partial\delta \\ -\partial F^2/\partial\delta \\ -\partial F^3/\partial\delta \end{bmatrix} = \begin{bmatrix} 0 \\ 0 \\ \overline{Y} \end{bmatrix}$$

(Note that $-\partial F^3/\partial\delta = Y = \overline{Y}$ when evaluated at the equilibrium.)

$$\text{Thus } \frac{\partial\overline{Y}}{\partial\delta} = \frac{\begin{vmatrix} 0 & -1 & 0 \\ 0 & 1 & \beta \\ \overline{Y} & 0 & 1 \end{vmatrix}}{|J|} = \frac{-\beta\overline{Y}}{1-\beta+\beta\delta}$$

These results do check with (7.20) and (7.21), respectively.

Exercise 8.6

1 (a) S' = marginal propensity to save; T' = marginal income tax rate;

I' = marginal propensity to invest.

(b) Writing the equilibrium condition as $F(Y; G_0) = S(Y) + T(Y) - I(Y) - G_0 = 0$, we find that F has continuous partial derivatives and $\partial F/\partial Y = S' + T' - I' \neq 0$. Thus the implicit-function theorem is applicable. The equilibrium identity is: $S(\overline{Y}) + T(\overline{Y}) - I(\overline{Y}) - G_0 \equiv 0$.

(c) By the implicit-function rule, we have

$$\left(\frac{d\overline{Y}}{dG_0}\right) = -\frac{-1}{S' + T' - I'} = \frac{1}{S' + T' - I'} > 0$$

An increase in G_0 will increase the equilibrium national income.

2 (a) $F(P; Y_0, T_0) = D(P, Y_0) - S(P, T_0) = 0$

(b) F has continuous partial derivatives, and $F_P = D_P - S_P \neq 0$, thus the implicit-function theorem is applicable. The equilibrium identity is: $D(\overline{P}, Y_0) - S(\overline{P}, T_0) \equiv 0$.

(c) By the implicit-function rule,

$$\left(\frac{\partial\overline{P}}{\partial Y_0}\right) = -\frac{D_{Y_0}}{D_{\overline{P}} - S_{\overline{P}}} > 0 \qquad \left(\frac{\partial\overline{P}}{\partial T_0}\right) = -\frac{-S_{T_0}}{D_{\overline{P}} - S_{\overline{P}}} > 0$$

An increase in income or taxes will raise the equilibrium price.

(d) The supply function implies $\overline{Q} = S(\overline{P}, T_0)$; thus $\left(\frac{\partial\overline{Q}}{\partial Y_0}\right) = \frac{\partial S}{\partial\overline{P}}\left(\frac{\partial\overline{P}}{\partial Y_0}\right) > 0$.

The demand function implies $\overline{Q} = D(\overline{P}, Y_0)$; thus $\left(\frac{\partial\overline{Q}}{\partial T_0}\right) = \frac{\partial D}{\partial\overline{P}}\left(\frac{\partial\overline{P}}{\partial T_0}\right) < 0$.

__Note:__ To use the demand function to get $(\partial\overline{Q}/\partial Y_0)$ would be more complicated, since Y_0 has both direct and indirect effects on $\overline{Q}_d$. A similar complication arises when the supply function is used to get the other comparative-static derivative.

3 Writing the equilibrium conditons as

$$F^1(P, Q; Y_0, T_0) = D(P, Y_0) - Q = 0$$

$$F^2(P, Q; Y_0, T_0) = S(P, T_0) - Q = 0$$

We find $|J| = \begin{vmatrix} D_P & -1 \\ S_P & -1 \end{vmatrix} = S_P - D_P \neq 0$. Thus the implicit-function theorem still applies, and we can write the equilibrium identities

$$D(\overline{P}, Y_0) - \overline{Q} \equiv 0$$

$$S(\overline{P}, T_0) - \overline{Q} \equiv 0$$

tal differentiation yields

$$D_{\overline{P}}\, d\overline{P} - d\overline{Q} = -D_{Y_0}\, dY_0$$

$$S_{\overline{P}}\, d\overline{P} - d\overline{Q} = \qquad - S_{T_0}\, dT_0$$

n Y_0 is the disequilibrating factor ($dT_0 = 0$), we have

$$\begin{bmatrix} D_{\overline{P}} & -1 \\ S_{\overline{P}} & -1 \end{bmatrix} \begin{bmatrix} (\partial\overline{P}/\partial Y_0) \\ (\partial\overline{Q}/\partial Y_0) \end{bmatrix} = \begin{bmatrix} -D_{Y_0} \\ 0 \end{bmatrix}$$

hus $\left(\dfrac{\partial\overline{P}}{\partial Y_0}\right) = \dfrac{D_{Y_0}}{S_{\overline{P}} - D_{\overline{P}}} > 0$ and $\left(\dfrac{\partial\overline{Q}}{\partial Y_0}\right) = \dfrac{D_{Y_0} S_{\overline{P}}}{S_{\overline{P}} - D_{\overline{P}}} > 0$

When T_0 is the disequilibrating factor ($dY_0 = 0$), we can similarly get $\left(\dfrac{\partial\overline{P}}{\partial T_0}\right) = \dfrac{-S_{T_0}}{S_{\overline{P}} - D_{\overline{P}}} > 0$ and $\left(\dfrac{\partial\overline{Q}}{\partial T_0}\right) = \dfrac{-S_{T_0} D_{\overline{P}}}{S_{\overline{P}} - D_{\overline{P}}} < 0$

(a) $F(P; t_0, Q_{s0}) = D(P, t_0) - Q_{s0} = 0$

(b) Since the partial derivatives of F are all continuous, and $F_P = \partial D/\partial P \neq 0$, the implicit-function theorem applies.

(c) To find $(\partial\overline{P}/\partial t_0)$, use the implicit-function rule on the equilibrium identity $D(\overline{P}, t_0) - Q_{s0} \equiv 0$, to get

$$\left(\frac{\partial\overline{P}}{\partial t_0}\right) = -\frac{\partial D/\partial t_0}{\partial D/\partial\overline{P}} > 0$$

An increase in consumers' taste will raise the equilibrium price.

5 Taking M_{s0} to be the disequilibrating factor, we can get from (8.41)

$$\begin{bmatrix} -S_Y - M' & I' - S_i \\ L_Y & L_i \end{bmatrix} \begin{bmatrix} (\partial \bar{Y}/\partial M_{s0}) \\ (\partial \bar{i}/\partial M_{s0}) \end{bmatrix} = \begin{bmatrix} 0 \\ 1 \end{bmatrix}$$

Thus, using the Jacobian in (8.39), we have the results

$$\left(\frac{\partial \bar{Y}}{\partial M_{s0}}\right) = \frac{-(I' - S_i)}{|J|} > 0, \qquad \left(\frac{\partial \bar{i}}{\partial M_{s0}}\right) = \frac{-(S_Y + M')}{|J|} < 0$$

An increase in the money supply raises the equilibrium income, but lowers the equilibrium interest rate.

6 (a) Yes. (b) $kY + L(i)$

(c) We can take the two equilibrium conditions as the equations $F^1 = 0$ and $F^2 = 0$, respectively. Since the Jacobian is nonzero:

$$|J| = \begin{vmatrix} \partial F^1/\partial Y & \partial F^1/\partial i \\ \partial F^2/\partial Y & \partial F^2/\partial i \end{vmatrix} = \begin{vmatrix} (1 - C') & -I' \\ k & L' \end{vmatrix}$$

$$= L'(1 - C') + kI' < 0$$

the implicit-function theorem applies, and we have the equilibrium identities

$$\bar{Y} - C(\bar{Y}) - I(\bar{i}) - G_0 \equiv 0$$

$$k\bar{Y} + L(\bar{i}) - M_{s0} \equiv 0$$

With M_{s0} as the disequilibrating factor, we can get the equation

$$\begin{bmatrix} (1 - C') & -I' \\ k & L' \end{bmatrix} \begin{bmatrix} (\partial \bar{Y}/\partial M_{s0}) \\ (\partial \bar{i}/\partial M_{s0}) \end{bmatrix} = \begin{bmatrix} 0 \\ 1 \end{bmatrix}$$

It follows that

$$\left(\frac{\partial \bar{Y}}{\partial M_{s0}}\right) = \frac{I'}{|J|} > 0 \quad \text{and} \quad \left(\frac{\partial \bar{i}}{\partial M_{s0}}\right) = \frac{1 - C'}{|J|} < 0$$

Next, taking G_0 to be the disequilibrating factor, we get

$$\begin{bmatrix} (1 - C') & -I' \\ k & L' \end{bmatrix} \begin{bmatrix} (\partial \bar{Y}/\partial G_0) \\ (\partial \bar{i}/\partial G_0) \end{bmatrix} = \begin{bmatrix} 1 \\ 0 \end{bmatrix}$$

This yields the results

$$\left(\frac{\partial \bar{Y}}{\partial G_0}\right) = \frac{L'}{|J|} > 0 \quad \text{and} \quad \left(\frac{\partial \bar{i}}{\partial G_0}\right) = -\frac{k}{|J|} > 0$$

CHAPTER 9

Exercise 9.2

(a) $f'(x) = -4x + 4 = 0$ iff $x = 1$; the stationary value $f(1) = 11$ is a relative maximum.

(b) $f'(x) = 10x + 1 = 0$ iff $x = -1/10$; $f(-1/10) = -1/20$ is a relative minimum.

(c) $f'(x) = 2x = 0$ iff $x = 0$; $f(0) = 3$ is a relative minimum.

(d) $f'(x) = 6x - 6 = 0$ iff $x = 1$; $f(1) = -1$ is a relative minimum.

(a) Setting $f'(x) = 3x^2 - 3 = 0$ yields two critical values, 1 and -1. The latter is outside the domain; the former leads to $f(1) = 3$, a relative minimum.

(b) The only critical value is $x = 1$; $f(1) = 10\frac{1}{3}$ is a point of inflection.

(c) Setting $f'(x) = -3x^2 + 9x - 6 = 0$ yields two critical values, 1 and 2; $f(1) = 3.5$ is a relative minimum but $f(2) = 4$ is a relative maximum.

When $x = 1$, we have $y = 2$ (a minimum); when $x = -1$, we have $y = -2$ (a maximum). These are in the nature of relative extrema, thus a minimum can exceed a maximum.

(a) $M = \phi'(x)$ $\qquad$ $A = \phi(x)/x$

(b) When A reaches a relative extremum, we must have

$$\frac{dA}{dx} = \frac{1}{x^2}[x\phi'(x) - \phi(x)] = 0$$

This occurs only when $x\phi'(x) = \phi(x)$, that is, only when $\phi'(x) = \phi(x)/x$, or only when $M = A$.

(c) The marginal and average curves must intersect when the latter reaches a peak or a trough.

(d) $\varepsilon = \frac{M}{A} = 1$ when $M = A$.

Exercise 9.3

1 (a) $f'(x) = 2ax + b$; $f''(x) = 2a$; $f'''(x) = 0$

(b) $f'(x) = 24x^3 - 3$; $f''(x) = 72x^2$; $f'''(x) = 144x$

(c) $f'(x) = 2(1 - x)^{-2}$; $f''(x) = 4(1 - x)^{-3}$; $f'''(x) = 12(1 - x)^{-4}$

(d) $f'(x) = 2(1 - x)^{-2}$; $f''(x) = 4(1 - x)^{-3}$; $f'''(x) = 12(1 - x)^{-4}$

2 (a) and (d).

3 (a) An example is a modified version of the curve in Fig. 9.5a, with the arc AB replaced by a line segment AB. (b) A straight line.

4 Since $dy/dx = b/(c + x)^2 > 0$, and $d^2y/dx^2 = -2b/(c + x)^3 < 0$, the curve must show y increasing at a decreasing rate. The vertical intercept (where $x = 0$) is $a - \frac{b}{c}$. When x approaches infinity, y tends to the value a, which gives a horizontal asymptote. Thus the range of the function is the interval $[a - \frac{b}{c}, a)$. To use it as a consumption function, we should stipulate that:

$a > \frac{b}{c}$ [so that consumption is positive at zero income]

$b < c^2$ [so that MPC = dy/dx is a positive fraction throughout]

5 The function f(x) plots as a straight line, and g(x) plots as a curve with either a peak or a bottom or an inflection point at $x = 3$. In terms of stationary points, every point on f(x) is a stationary point, but the only stationary point on g(x) we know of is at $x = 3$.

Exercise 9.4

1 (a) $f'(x) = -4x + 8$; $f''(x) = -4$. The critical value is $x = 2$; the stationary value $f(2) = 33$ is a maximum.

(b) $f'(x) = 3x^2 + 12x$; $f''(x) = 6x + 12$. The critical values are 0 and -4. $f(0) = 7$ is a minimum, because $f''(0) = 12 > 0$, but $f(-4) = 39$ is a maximum, because $f''(-4) = -12 < 0$.

(c) $f'(x) = x^2 - 6x + 5$; $f''(x) = 2x - 6$. The critical values are 1 and 5. $f(1) = 5\frac{1}{3}$ is a maximum because $f''(1) = -4$, but $f(5) = -5\frac{1}{3}$ is a minimum because $f''(5) = 4$.

(d) $f'(x) = 2/(1 - 2x)^2 \neq 0$ for any value of x; there exists no relative extremum.

Excluding the wall side, the other three sides must satisfy $L + 2W = 32$ ft, or $L = 32 - 2W$. The area is therefore

$$A = WL = W(32 - 2W) = 32W - 2W^2$$

o maximize A, it is necessary that $dA/dW = 32 - 4W = 0$, which can ccur only when $W = 8$. Thus

$$\overline{W} = 8 \text{ ft} \qquad \overline{L} = 32 - 2\overline{W} = 16 \text{ ft} \qquad \overline{A} = \overline{WL} = 128 \text{ ft}^2$$

nasmuch as $d^2A/dW^2 = -4$ is negative, $\overline{A}$ is a maximum.

a) Yes.

b) From the demand function, we first get the AR function $P = 100 - Q$. Then we have $R = PQ = (100 - Q)Q = 100Q - Q^2$.

c) $\pi = R - C = -\frac{1}{3}Q^3 + 6Q^2 - 11Q - 50$

d) Setting $d\pi/dQ = -Q^2 + 12Q - 11 = 0$ yields two critical values 1 and 11. Only $\overline{Q} = 11$ gives a maximum profit.

(e) Maximum profit $= 111\frac{1}{3}$

If $b = 0$, then the MC-minimizing output level becomes $Q^* = -\frac{b}{3a} = 0$. With its minimum at zero output, the MC curve must be upward-sloping throughout. Since the increasing segment of MC is associated with the convex segment of the C curve, $b = 0$ implies that the C curve will be convex throughout.

(a) The first assumption means $\pi(0) < 0$. Since $\pi(0) = k$, we need the restriction $k < 0$.

(b) Strict concavity means $\pi''(Q) < 0$. Since $\pi''(Q) = 2h$, we should have $h < 0$.

(c) The third assumption means $\pi'(\bar{Q}) = 0$, or $2h\bar{Q} + j = 0$. Since $\bar{Q} = -j/2h$, and since $h < 0$, the positivity of $\bar{Q}$ requires that $j > 0$.

6 (a) $Q = f(L)$; $R = P_0Q = P_0f(L)$; $C = W_0L + F$; $\pi = R - C = P_0f(L) - W_0L - F$

(b) $d\pi/dL = P_0f'(L) - W_0 = 0$, or $P_0f'(L) = W_0$. The value of marginal product must be equated to the wage rate.

(c) $d^2\pi/dL^2 = P_0f''(L)$. If $f''(L) < 0$ (diminishing MPP_L), then we can be sure that profit is maximized by $\bar{L}$.

7 (a) $S = \frac{d}{dQ} AR = -23 + 2.2Q - 0.054Q^2$

(b) $\frac{dS}{dQ} = 2.2 - 0.108Q = 0$ at $Q^* = 20.37$ (approximately); since

$\frac{d^2S}{dQ^2} = -0.108 < 0$, Q^* will maximize S.

$$S_{max} = S|_{Q=Q^*} = -23 + 2.2(20.37) - 0.054(20.37)^2$$
$$= -0.59 \text{ (approximately).}$$

(c) Since S_{max} is negative, all S values must be negative.

Exercise 9.5

1 (a) 120 (b) 5040 (c) $\frac{4(3!)}{3!} = 4$

(d) $\frac{(6)(5)(4)(3!)}{3!} = 6 \cdot 5 \cdot 4 = 120$

(e) $\frac{(n+2)(n+1)n!}{n!} = (n+2)(n+1)$

2 (a)

$$\begin{aligned} \phi(x) &= (1-x)^{-1} & \text{so that} \quad \phi(0) &= 1 \\ \phi'(x) &= (1-x)^{-2} & \phi'(0) &= 1 \\ \phi''(x) &= 2(1-x)^{-3} & \phi''(0) &= 2 \\ \phi'''(x) &= 6(1-x)^{-4} & \phi'''(0) &= 6 \\ \phi^{(4)}(x) &= 24(1-x)^{-5} & \phi^{(4)}(0) &= 24 \end{aligned}$$

Thus, according to (9.14), the first five terms are

$$1 + x + x^2 + x^3 + x^4$$

(b) $\phi(x) = (1 - x)/(1 + x)$ so that $\phi(0) = 1$

$\phi'(x) = -2(1 + x)^{-2}$ $\qquad \phi'(0) = -2$

$\phi''(x) = 4(1 + x)^{-3}$ $\qquad \phi''(0) = 4$

$\phi'''(x) = -12(1 + x)^{-4}$ $\qquad \phi'''(0) = -12$

$\phi^{(4)}(x) = 48(1 + x)^{-5}$ $\qquad \phi^{(4)}(0) = 48$

Thus, by (9.14), the first five terms are

$$1 - 2x + 2x^2 - 2x^3 + 2x^4$$

a) $\phi(-2) = 1/3$, $\phi'(-2) = 1/9$, $\phi''(-2) = 2/27$, $\phi'''(-2) = 6/81$, and $\phi^{(4)}(-2) = 24/243$. Thus, by (9.14),

$$\phi(x) = \frac{1}{3} + \frac{1}{9}(x + 2) + \frac{1}{27}(x + 2)^2 + \frac{1}{81}(x + 2)^3 + \frac{1}{243}(x + 2)^4 + R_4$$

$$= \frac{1}{243}(211 + 131x + 51x^2 + 11x^3 + x^4) + R_4$$

b) $\phi(-2) = -3$, $\phi'(-2) = -2$, $\phi''(-2) = -4$, $\phi'''(-2) = -12$, and $\phi^{(4)}(-2) = -48$. Thus, by (9.14),

$$\phi(x) = -3 - 2(x + 2) - 2(x + 2)^2 - 2(x + 2)^3 - 2(x + 2)^4 + R_4$$

$$= -63 - 98x - 62x^2 - 18x^3 - 2x^4 + R_4$$

When $x = x_0$, all the terms on the right of (9.14) except the first one will drop out (including R_n), leaving the result $\phi(x) = \phi(x_0)$.

ercise 9.6

(a) $f'(x) = 3x^2 = 0$ only when $x = 0$, thus $f(0) = 0$ is the only stationary value. The first nonzero derivative value is $f'''(0) = 6$; so $f(0)$ is an inflection point.

(b) $f'(x) = -4x^3 = 0$ only when $x = 0$. The stationary value $f(0) = 0$ is a relative maximum because the first nonzero derivative value is $f^{(4)}(0) = -24$.

(c) $f'(x) = 6x^5 = 0$ only when $x = 0$. The stationary value $f(0) = 5$ is a relative minimum since the first nonzero derivative value is $f^{(6)}(0) = 720$.

2 (a) $f'(x) = 3(x - 1)^2 = 0$ only when $x = 1$. The first nonzero derivative value is $f'''(1) = 6$. Thus the stationary value $f(1) = 16$ is associated with an inflection point.

(b) $f'(x) = 4(x - 2)^3 = 0$ only when $x = 2$. Since the first nonzero derivative value is $f^{(4)}(2) = 24$, the stationary value $f(2) = 0$ is a relative minimum.

(c) $f'(x) = -6(3 - x)^5 = 0$ only when $x = 3$. Since the first nonzero derivative is $f^{(6)}(3) = 720$, the stationary value $f(3) = 7$ is a relative minimum.

CHAPTER 10

ercise 10.1

(a) Yes. (b) Yes, because at $t = 0$, the value

f y for the two functions are identical: $3^0 = 1$, and $3^{2(0)} = 1$.

a) Yes. (b) No, because at $t = 0$, the value

f y for the two functions are unequal: $4^0 = 1$, but $3(4^0) = 3$.

a) Let $w = 5t$ (so that $dw/dt = 5$), then $y = e^w$ and $dy/dw = e^w$.

ius, by the chain rule, $\frac{dy}{dt} = \frac{dy}{dw}\frac{dw}{dt} = 5e^w = 5e^{5t}$.

) Let $w = 3t$, then $y = 4e^w$ and $dy/dw = 4e^w$. Thus we have

$$\frac{dy}{dt} = \frac{dy}{dw}\frac{dw}{dt} = 12e^w = 12e^{3t}$$

Similarly to (b) above, $dy/dt = -12e^{-2t}$.

first two derivatives are $y'(t) = y''(t) = e^t = (2.718)^t$. The

ue of t can be either positive, zero, or negative. If $t > 0$,

en e^t is clearly positive; if $t = 0$, then $e^t = 1$, again positive;

nally, if $t < 0$, say $t = -2$, then $e^t = 1/(2.718)^2$, still positive.

hus $y'(t)$ and $y''(t)$ are always positive, and the function $y = e^t$

always increases at an increasing rate.

(a) The curve with $a = -1$ is the mirror image of the curve with $a = 1$ with reference to the horizontal exis.

(b) The curve with $c = -1$ is the mirror image of the curve with $c = 1$ with reference to the vertical axis.

ercise 10.2

(a) $e^2 = 1 + 2 + \frac{1}{2}(2)^2 + \frac{1}{6}(2)^3 + \frac{1}{24}(2)^4 + \frac{1}{120}(2)^5 + \frac{1}{720}(2)^6$

$$+ \frac{1}{5040}(2)^7 + \frac{1}{40320}(2)^8 + \frac{1}{362880}(2)^9 + \frac{1}{3628800}(2)^{10}$$

$$= 1 + 2 + 2 + 1.333 + 0.667 + 0.267 + 0.089 + 0.025$$

$$+ 0.006 + 0.001 + 0.000 = 7.388$$

(b) $e^{1/2} = 1 + \frac{1}{2} + \frac{1}{2}(\frac{1}{2})^2 + \frac{1}{6}(\frac{1}{2})^3 + \frac{1}{24}(\frac{1}{2})^4 + \frac{1}{120}(\frac{1}{2})^5$

$= 1 + 0.5 + 0.125 + 0.021 + 0.003 + 0.000 = 1.649$

2 (a) The derivatives are: $\phi' = 2e^{2x}$, $\phi'' = 2^2e^{2x}$, $\phi''' = 2^3e^{2x}$, or in general $\phi^{(k)} = 2^ke^{2x}$. Thus we have $\phi'(0) = 2$, $\phi''(0) = 2^2$, or more generally $\phi^{(k)}(0) = 2^k$. Accordingly,

$$P_n = 1 + 2x + \frac{1}{2!}2^2x^2 + \frac{1}{3!}2^3x^3 + \ldots + \frac{1}{n!}2^nx^n$$

$$= 1 + 2x + \frac{1}{2!}(2x)^2 + \frac{1}{3!}(2x)^3 + \ldots + \frac{1}{n!}(2x)^n$$

(b) $R_n = \dfrac{\phi^{(n+1)}(p)}{(n+1)!}x^{n+1} = \dfrac{2^{n+1}e^{2p}}{(n+1)!}x^{n+1} = \dfrac{e^{2p}}{(n+1)!}(2x)^{n+1}$

It can be verified that $R_n \to 0$ as $n \to \infty$.

(c) Hence $\phi(x)$ can be expressed as an infinite series:

$$\phi(x) = 1 + 2x + \frac{1}{2!}(2x)^2 + \frac{1}{3!}(2x)^3 + \ldots$$

3 (a) $\$10e^{0.05(3)} = \$10e^{0.15}$ (b) $\$690e^{0.04(2)} = \$690e^{0.08}$

4 (a) 0.07 (or 7%) (b) 0.03 (c) 0.20 (d) 1 (or 100%)

5 When $t = 0$, the two functions have the same value (the same y intercept). Also, $y_1 = Ae^r$ when $t = 1$, but $y_2 = Ae^r$ when $t = -1$. Generally, $y_1 = y_2$ whenever the value of t in one function is the negative of the t value in the other; hence the mirror-image relationship.

Exercise 10.3

1 (a) 4 (b) -4 (c) 4 (d) 5

2 (a) 2 (b) -4 (c) -3 (d) -2 (e) 6 (f) 0

3 (a) $\log_{10}(100)^{14} = 14\log_{10}100 = 14(2) = 28$

(b) $\log_{10}(\frac{1}{100}) = \log_{10}1 - \log_{10}100 = 0 - 2 = -2$

(c) $\ln\frac{3}{B} = \ln 3 - \ln B$

(d) $\ln Ae^2 = \ln A + \ln e^2 = \ln A + 2$

(e) $\ln ABe^{-4} = \ln A + \ln B + \ln e^{-4} = \ln A + \ln B - 4$

(f) $(\log_4 e)(\log_e 64) = \log_4 64 = 3$

(a) and (c) are valid; (b) and (d) are not.

By definition, $e^{\ln (u/v)} = \frac{u}{v}$. But we can also write

$\frac{u}{v} = \frac{e^{\ln u}}{e^{\ln v}} = e^{(\ln u - \ln v)}$. Equating the two expressions for $\frac{u}{v}$,

we obtain $\ln \frac{u}{v} = \ln u - \ln v$.

rcise 10.4

f $r = 0$, then $y = Ae^{rt} = Ae^{0} = A$, and the function degenerates

nto a constant function. The nonzero requirement serves to

reclude this contingency.

ie graphs are of the same general shape as in Fig. 10.3; the y

tercepts will be A (i.e., $y = A$) for both.

ince $y = ab^{ct}$, we have $\log_b y = \log_b a + ct \log_b b = \log_b a + ct$.

hus, by solving for t, we get

$$t = \frac{\log_b y - \log_b a}{c} \qquad (c \neq 0)$$

This is the desired inverse function because it expresses t in

erms of y.

(a) $a = 1$, $b = 8$, and $c = 3$; thus $r = 3 \ln 8$, and $y = e^{(3 \ln 8)t}$.

We can also write this as $y = e^{6.2385t}$.

(b) $a = 2$, $b = 7$, and $c = 2$; thus $r = 2 \ln 7$, and $y = 2e^{(2 \ln 7)t}$.

We can also write this as $y = 2e^{3.8918t}$.

(c) $a = 5$, $b = 5$, and $c = 1$; thus $r = \ln 5$, and $y = 5e^{(\ln 5)t}$.

We can also write this as $y = 5e^{1.6095t}$.

(d) $a = 2$, $b = 15$, and $c = 4$; thus $r = 4 \ln 15$, and $y = 2e^{(4 \ln 15)t}$.

We can also write this as $y = 2e^{10.8324t}$.

5 (a) $a = 1$, $b = 7$, $c = 1$; thus

$$t = \frac{1}{\ln 7} \ln y \; (= \frac{1}{1.9459} \ln y = 0.5139 \ln y)$$

(b) $a = 1$, $b = 8$, $c = 3$; thus

$$t = \frac{1}{\ln 8} \ln 3y \; (= \frac{1}{2.0795} \ln 3y = 0.4809 \ln 3y)$$

(c) $a = 3$, $b = 15$, $c = 9$; thus

$$t = \frac{3}{\ln 15} \ln 9y \; (= \frac{3}{2.7081} \ln 9y = 1.1078 \ln 9y)$$

(d) $a = 2$, $b = 10$, $c = 1$; thus

$$t = \frac{2}{\ln 10} \ln y \; (= \frac{2}{2.3026} \ln y = 0.8686 \ln y)$$

6 The conversion involved is $Ae^{rt} = A(1 + \frac{i}{c})^{ct}$, where c represents the number of compoundings per year. Similarly to formula (10.18), we can obtain a general conversion formula $r = c \ln (1 + \frac{i}{c})$.

(a) $c = 1$ and $i = 0.05$; thus $r = \ln 1.05$.

(b) $c = 2$ and $i = 0.05$; thus $r = 2 \ln 1.025$.

(c) $c = 2$ and $i = 0.06$; thus $r = 2 \ln 1.03$.

(d) $c = 4$ and $i = 0.06$; thus $r = 4 \ln 1.015$.

Exercise 10.5

1 (a) $2e^{2t+4}$ (b) $-7e^{1-7t}$ (c) $2te^{t^2+1}$

(d) $-6te^{2-t^2}$ (e) $(2ax + b)e^{2x^2+bx+c}$

(f) $\frac{dy}{dx} = x \frac{d}{dx} e^x + e^x \frac{dx}{dx} = xe^x + e^x = (x + 1)e^x$

(g) $\frac{dy}{dx} = x^2(2e^{2x}) + 2xe^{2x} = 2x(x + 1)e^{2x}$

(h) $\frac{dy}{dx} = a(xbe^{bx+c} + e^{bx+c}) = a(bx + 1)e^{bx+c}$

2 (a) $\frac{d}{dt} \ln at = \frac{d}{dt} (\ln a + \ln t) = 0 + \frac{d}{dt} \ln t = \frac{1}{t}$

(b) $\frac{d}{dt} \ln t^c = \frac{d}{dt} c \ln t = c \frac{d}{dt} \ln t = \frac{c}{t}$

3 (a) $\frac{dy}{dt} = \frac{40t^4}{8t^5} = \frac{5}{t}$ (b) $\frac{dy}{dt} = \frac{act^{c-1}}{at^c} = \frac{c}{t}$

(c) $\frac{dy}{dt} = \frac{1}{t + 9}$ (d) $\frac{dy}{dt} = 5 \frac{2(t + 1)}{(t + 1)^2} = \frac{10}{t + 1}$

(e) $\frac{dy}{dx} = \frac{1}{x} - \frac{1}{1 + x} = \frac{1}{x(1 + x)}$

(f) $\frac{dy}{dx} = \frac{d}{dx}[\ln x + 8 \ln (1 - x)] = \frac{1}{x} + \frac{-8}{1 - x} = \frac{1 - 9x}{x(1 - x)}$

(g) $\frac{dy}{dx} = \frac{d}{dx}[\ln 3x - \ln (1 + x)] = \frac{3}{3x} - \frac{1}{1 + x} = \frac{1}{x(1 + x)}$

(h) $\frac{dy}{dx} = 5x^4 \frac{2x}{x^2} + 20x^3 \ln x^2 = 10x^3 (1 + 2 \ln x^2) = 10x^3(1 + 4 \ln x)$

(a) $\frac{dy}{dt} = 5^t \ln 5$

(b) $\frac{dy}{dt} = \frac{1}{(t + 1) \ln 2}$

(c) $\frac{dy}{dt} = 2(13)^{2t+3} \ln 13$

(d) $\frac{dy}{dx} = \frac{14x}{7x^2} \frac{1}{\ln 7} = \frac{2}{x \ln 7}$

(e) $\frac{dy}{dx} = \frac{16x}{(8x^2 + 3) \ln 2}$

(f) $\frac{dy}{dx} = x^2 \frac{d}{dx} \log_3 x + \log_3 x \frac{d}{dx} x^2$

$$= x^2 \frac{1}{x \ln 3} + (\log_3 x)(2x) = \frac{x}{\ln 3} + 2x \log_3 x$$

(a) Let $u = f(t)$, so that $du/dt = f'(t)$. Then

$$\frac{d}{dt} b^{f(t)} = \frac{db^u}{dt} = \frac{db^u}{du}\frac{du}{dt} = (b^u \ln b)f'(t) = f'(t)b^{f(t)} \ln b$$

(b) Let $u = f(t)$. Then

$$\frac{d}{dt} \log_b f(t) = \frac{d}{dt} \log_b u = \frac{d}{du} \log_b u \frac{du}{dt} = \frac{1}{u \ln b} f'(t)$$

$$= \frac{f'(t)}{f(t)} \frac{1}{\ln b}$$

For $V = Ae^{rt}$, the first two derivatives are

$$V' = rAe^{rt} > 0 \qquad \text{and} \qquad V'' = r^2Ae^{rt} > 0$$

Thus V increases monotonically at an increasing rate, yielding a strictly convex curve. For $A = Ve^{-rt}$, the first two derivatives are

$$A' = -rVe^{-rt} < 0 \qquad \text{and} \qquad A'' = r^2Ve^{-rt} > 0$$

Thus A decreases monotonically at an increasing rate (with the negative slope taking smaller numerical values as t increases), also yielding a strictly convex curve.

7 (a) Since $\ln y = \ln 3x - \ln (x + 2) - \ln (x + 4)$, we have

$$\frac{1}{y}\frac{dy}{dx} = \frac{1}{x} - \frac{1}{x + 2} - \frac{1}{x + 4} = \frac{8 - x^2}{x(x + 2)(x + 4)}$$

and $\frac{dy}{dx} = \frac{8 - x^2}{x(x + 2)(x + 4)} \frac{3x}{(x + 2)(x + 4)} = \frac{3(8 - x^2)}{(x + 2)^2(x + 4)^2}$

(b) Since $\ln y = \ln (x^2 + 3) + x^2 + 1$, we have

$$\frac{1}{y} \frac{dy}{dx} = \frac{2x}{x^2 + 3} + 2x = \frac{2x(x^2 + 4)}{x^2 + 3}$$

and $\frac{dy}{dx} = \frac{2x(x^2 + 4)}{x^2 + 3}(x^2 + 3)e^{x^2+1} = 2x(x^2 + 4)e^{x^2+1}$

Exercise 10.6

1 Since $A = Ke^{2\sqrt{t}-rt}$, we have $\ln A = \ln K + 2\sqrt{t} - rt$. Differentiation with respect to t yields

$$\frac{1}{A} \frac{dA}{dt} = t^{-1/2} - r \qquad \text{or} \qquad \frac{dA}{dt} = A(t^{-1/2} - r)$$

Setting $dA/dt = 0$, we then find: $\bar{t} = 1/r^2$.

In the second derivative,

$$\frac{d^2A}{dt^2} = A \frac{d}{dt}(t^{-1/2} - r) + (t^{-1/2} - r)\frac{dA}{dt}$$

the second term vanishes when $dA/dt = 0$. Thus $d^2A/dt^2 = -A/2\sqrt{t^3} < 0$, which satisfies the second-order condition for a maximum.

2 $\frac{d^2A}{dt^2} = A \frac{d}{dt}\left(\frac{\ln 2}{2\sqrt{t}} - r\right) + \left(\frac{\ln 2}{2\sqrt{t}} - r\right)\frac{dA}{dt} = A\frac{d}{dt}\left(\frac{\ln 2}{2} t^{-1/2} - r\right) + 0$ [since $dA/dt = 0$]

$= \frac{-A \ln 2}{4\sqrt{t^3}} < 0$ [since $A > 0$ and $\ln 2 > 0$]

Thus the second-order condition is satisfied.

3 (a) Since $A = Ve^{-rt} = f(t)e^{-rt}$, we have $\ln A = \ln f(t) - rt$, and

$$\frac{1}{A} \frac{dA}{dt} = \frac{f'(t)}{f(t)} - r = r_v - r \qquad \text{or} \qquad \frac{dA}{dt} = A(r_v - r)$$

Inasmuch as A is nonzero, $dA/dt = 0$ if and only if $r_v = r$.

(b) The second derivative is

$$\frac{d^2A}{dt^2} = A \frac{d}{dt} \frac{f'(t)}{f(t)} = A \frac{d}{dt} r_v < 0 \qquad \text{iff} \qquad \frac{d}{dt} r_v < 0$$

Exercise 10.7

1 (a) $\ln y = \ln 3 + 2 \ln t$; thus $r_y = \frac{d}{dt} \ln y = \frac{2}{t}$.

(b) $\ln y = \ln a + c \ln t$; thus $r_y = c/t$.

(c) $\ln y = \ln a + t \ln b$; thus $r_y = \ln b$.

(d) Let $u = 2^t$ and $v = t^2$. Then $r_u = \ln 2$, and $r_v = 2/t$. Thus $r_y = r_u + r_v = \ln 2 + 2/t$. Alternatively, we can write $\ln y = t \ln 2 + 2 \ln t$; thus $r_y = \frac{d}{dt} \ln y = \ln 2 + \frac{2}{t}$

(e) Let $u = t$ and $v = 3^t$. Then $r_u = \frac{d(\ln u)}{dt} = \frac{d(\ln t)}{dt} = \frac{1}{t}$, and $r_v = \frac{d(\ln v)}{dt} = \frac{d(\ln 3^t)}{dt} = \frac{d(t \ln c)}{dt} = \ln 3$. Consequently, $r_y = r_u - r_v = \frac{1}{t} - \ln 3$. Alternatively, we can write $\ln y = \ln t - t \ln 3$; thus

$$r_y = \frac{d}{dt} \ln y = \frac{1}{t} - \ln 3$$

$\ln H = \ln H_0 + bt \ln 2$; thus $r_H = b \ln 2$. Similarly, $\ln C = \ln C_0 + at \ln e$; thus $r_C = a \ln e = a$. It follows that $r_{(C/H)} = r_C - r_H = a - b \ln 2$.

Taking log, we get $\ln y = k \ln x$. Differentiating with respect to t, we then obtain $r_y = k\, r_x$.

$y = \frac{u}{v}$ implies $\ln y = \ln u - \ln v$; it follows that

$$r_y = \frac{d}{dt} \ln y = \frac{d}{dt} \ln u - \frac{d}{dt} \ln v = r_u - r_v$$

$z = u - v$ implies $\ln z = \ln (u - v)$; thus

$$r_z = \frac{d}{dt} \ln z = \frac{d}{dt} \ln (u - v) = \frac{1}{u - v} \frac{d}{dt}(u - v)$$

$$= \frac{1}{u - v}[f'(t) - g'(t)] = \frac{1}{u - v} (ur_u - vr_v)$$

6 $\ln Q_d = \ln k - n \ln P$. Thus, by (10.28), $\varepsilon_d = -n$, and $|\varepsilon_d| = n$.

7 (a) Since $\ln y = \ln w + \ln z$, we have

$$\varepsilon_{yx} = \frac{d(\ln y)}{d(\ln x)} = \frac{d(\ln w)}{d(\ln x)} + \frac{d(\ln z)}{d(\ln x)} = \varepsilon_{wx} + \varepsilon_{zx}$$

(b) Since $\ln y = \ln u - \ln v$, we have

$$\varepsilon_{yx} = \frac{d(\ln y)}{d(\ln x)} = \frac{d(\ln u)}{d(\ln x)} - \frac{d(\ln v)}{d(\ln x)} = \varepsilon_{ux} - \varepsilon_{vx}$$

8 Let $u = \log_b y$, and $v = \log_b x$ (implying that $x = b^v$). Then

$$\frac{du}{dv} = \frac{du}{dy}\frac{dy}{dx}\frac{dx}{dv} = \frac{1}{y}(\log_b e)\frac{dy}{dx} b^v \ln b$$

Since $\log_b e = \frac{1}{\ln b}$, and since $b^v = x$, we have

$$\frac{du}{dv} = \frac{x}{y}\frac{dy}{dx} = \varepsilon_{yx}$$

9 Since $M_d = f[Y(t), i(t)]$, we can write the total derivative

$$\frac{dM_d}{dt} = f_y \frac{dY}{dt} + f_i \frac{di}{dt}$$

Thus the rate of growth of M_d is

$$r_{M_d} = \frac{dM_d/dt}{M_d} = \frac{f_Y}{f}\frac{dY}{dt} + \frac{f_i}{f}\frac{di}{dt} = \frac{f_Y}{f}\frac{Y}{Y}\frac{dY}{dt} + \frac{f_i}{f}\frac{i}{i}\frac{di}{dt}$$

$$= \frac{f_Y Y}{f}\left(\frac{1}{Y}\frac{dY}{dt}\right) + \frac{f_i i}{f}\left(\frac{1}{i}\frac{di}{dt}\right) = \varepsilon_{M_d Y}\, r_Y + \varepsilon_{M_d i}\, r_i$$

Alternatively, using logarithms, we may write $r_{M_d} = \frac{d}{dt}\ln M_d$ $= \frac{1}{M_d}\frac{d}{dt}M_d$, but this then leads us back to the preceding process.

10 By the same procedure used in 9 above, we can find that

$$r_Q = \varepsilon_{QK}\, r_K + \varepsilon_{QL}\, r_L$$

CHAPTER 11

Exercise 11.2

1 The derivatives are: $f_x = 2x + y$, $f_y = x + 4y$, $f_{xx} = 2$, $f_{yy} = 4$, and $f_{xy} = 1$. The first-order condition requires that $2x + y = 0$ and $x + 4y = 0$. Thus we have

$$\bar{x} = \bar{y} = 0 \qquad \text{implying} \qquad \bar{z} = 3 \text{ (which is a minimum)}$$

The derivatives are: $f_x = -2x + y + 2$, $f_y = x - 2y + 1$, $f_{xx} = -2$, $f_{yy} = -2$, and $f_{xy} = 1$. The first-order condition requires that $-2x + y = -2$ and $x - 2y = -1$. Thus we find

$$\bar{x} = \frac{5}{3} \qquad \bar{y} = \frac{4}{3} \qquad \text{so that} \qquad \bar{z} = \frac{7}{3} \text{ (which is a maximum)}$$

$f_x = 2ax$, $f_y = 2by$, $f_{xx} = 2a$, $f_{yy} = 2b$, and $f_{xy} = 0$. The first-order conditon requires that $2ax = 0$ and $2by = 0$. Thus

$$\bar{x} = \bar{y} = 0 \qquad \text{so that} \qquad \bar{z} = c$$

The second derivatives give us $f_{xx}f_{yy} = 4ab$, and $f_{xy}^2 = 0$. Thus:

(a) $\bar{z}$ is a minimum if $a, b > 0$. (b) $\bar{z}$ is a maximum if $a, b < 0$.

(c) $\bar{z}$ gives a saddle point if a and b have opposite signs.

$f_x = 2(e^{2x} - 1)$, $f_y = 4y$, $f_{xx} = 4e^{2x}$, $f_{yy} = 4$, and $f_{xy} = 0$. The first-order condition requires that $e^{2x} = 1$ and $4y = 0$. Thus

$$\bar{x} = \bar{y} = 0 \qquad \text{so that} \qquad \bar{z} = 4$$

Since $f_{xx}f_{yy} = 4(4)$ exceeds $f_{xy}^2 = 0$, $\bar{z} = 4$ is a minimum.

(a) Any pair (x, y) other than (2, 3) yields a positive z value.

(b) Yes. At $\bar{x} = 2$ and $\bar{y} = 3$, we find

$$f_x = 4(x - 2)^3 = 0 \qquad \text{and} \qquad f_y = 4(y - 3)^3 = 0$$

(c) No. At $\bar{x} = 2$ and $\bar{y} = 3$, we have $f_{xx} = f_{yy} = f_{xy} = f_{yx} = 0$.

(d) By (11.6), $d^2z = 0$. Thus (11.9) is satisfied.

Exercise 11.3

1 (a) $q = 4u^2 + 4uv + 3v^2$ (b) $q = -2u^2 + 4uv - 4v^2$

(c) $q = 5x^2 + 6xy$ (d) $q = f_{xx}\,dx^2 + 2f_{xy}\,dx\,dy + f_{yy}\,dy^2$

2 For (b): $q = -2u^2 + 4uv - 4v^2$. For (c): $q = 5x^2 + 6xy$. **Both are the same as before.**

3 (a) $\begin{bmatrix} 4 & 2 \\ 2 & 3 \end{bmatrix}$: $4 > 0$, $4(3) > 2^2$ ---positive definite

(b) $\begin{bmatrix} -2 & 2 \\ 2 & -4 \end{bmatrix}$: $-2 < 0$, $-2(-4) > 2^2$ ---negative definite

(c) $\begin{bmatrix} 5 & 3 \\ 3 & 0 \end{bmatrix}$: $5 > 0$, $5(0) < 3^2$ --- neither

4 (a) $q = [u \quad v]\begin{bmatrix} 3 & -2 \\ -2 & 7 \end{bmatrix}\begin{bmatrix} u \\ v \end{bmatrix}$ (b) $q = [u \quad v]\begin{bmatrix} 1 & 3.5 \\ 3.5 & 3 \end{bmatrix}\begin{bmatrix} u \\ v \end{bmatrix}$

(c) $q = [u \quad v]\begin{bmatrix} -1 & 4 \\ 4 & -31 \end{bmatrix}\begin{bmatrix} u \\ v \end{bmatrix}$ (d) $q = [x \quad y]\begin{bmatrix} -2 & 3 \\ 3 & -5 \end{bmatrix}\begin{bmatrix} x \\ y \end{bmatrix}$

(e) $q = [u_1 \quad u_2 \quad u_3]\begin{bmatrix} 3 & -1 & 2 \\ -1 & 5 & -1 \\ 2 & -1 & 4 \end{bmatrix}\begin{bmatrix} u_1 \\ u_2 \\ u_3 \end{bmatrix}$

(f) $q = [u \quad v \quad w]\begin{bmatrix} -1 & 2 & -3 \\ 2 & -4 & 0 \\ -3 & 0 & -7 \end{bmatrix}\begin{bmatrix} u \\ v \\ w \end{bmatrix}$

5 (a) $3 > 0$, $3(7) > (-2)^2$ ---positive definite

(b) $1 > 0$, $1(3) < (3.5)^2$ ---neither

(c) $-1 < 0$, $-1(-31) > 4^2$ ---negative definite

(d) $-2 < 0$, $-2(-5) > 3^2$ ---negative definite

(e) $3 > 0$, $\begin{vmatrix} 3 & -1 \\ -1 & 5 \end{vmatrix} = 14 > 0$, $\begin{vmatrix} 3 & -1 & 2 \\ -1 & 5 & -1 \\ 2 & -1 & 4 \end{vmatrix} = 37 > 0$

---positive definite

(f) $-1 < 0$, $\begin{vmatrix} -1 & 2 \\ 2 & -4 \end{vmatrix} = 0$ ---neither (no need to check $|D_3|$)

6 (a) The characteristic equation is

$$\begin{vmatrix} 4 - r & 2 \\ 2 & 3 - r \end{vmatrix} = r^2 - 7r + 8 = 0$$

Its roots are $r_1, r_2 = \frac{1}{2}(7 \pm \sqrt{17})$. Both roots being positive, $u'Du$ is positive definite.

(b) The characteristic equation is $r^2 + 6r + 4 = 0$, with roots

$r_1, r_2 = -3 \pm \sqrt{5}$. Both roots being negative, u'Eu is negative definite.

(c) The characteristic equation is $r^2 - 5r - 9 = 0$, with roots $r_1, r_2 = \frac{1}{2}(5 \pm \sqrt{61})$. Since r_1 is positive, but r_2 is negative, u'Fu is indefinite.

7 The characteristic equation $\begin{vmatrix} 4-r & 2 \\ 2 & 1-r \end{vmatrix} = r^2 - 5r = 0$ has the roots $r_1 = 5$ and $r_2 = 0$. (Note: This is an example where $|D| = 0$.) Using r_1 in (11.13'), we have $\begin{bmatrix} -1 & 2 \\ 2 & -4 \end{bmatrix}\begin{bmatrix} x_1 \\ x_2 \end{bmatrix} = 0$. Thus $x_1 = 2x_2$. Upon normalization, we obtain the first characteristic vector

$$v_1 = \begin{bmatrix} 2/\sqrt{5} \\ 1/\sqrt{5} \end{bmatrix}$$

Next, using r_2 in (11.13'), we have $\begin{bmatrix} 4 & 2 \\ 2 & 1 \end{bmatrix}\begin{bmatrix} x_1 \\ x_2 \end{bmatrix} = 0$. Therefore, $x_1 = -\frac{1}{2}x_2$. Upon normalization, we obtain

$$v_2 = \begin{bmatrix} -1/\sqrt{5} \\ 2/\sqrt{5} \end{bmatrix}$$

These results happen to be identical with those in Example 5.

8 The characteristic equation can be written as

$$r^2 - (d_{11} + d_{22})r + (d_{11}d_{22} - d_{12}d_{21}) = 0$$

Thus $r_1, r_2 = \frac{1}{2}[(d_{11} + d_{22}) \pm \sqrt{(d_{11} + d_{22})^2 - 4(d_{11}d_{22} - d_{12}d_{21})}]$

(a) The expression under the square-root sign can be written as

$$E = d_{11}^2 + 2d_{11}d_{22} + d_{22}^2 - 4d_{11}d_{22} + 4d_{12}d_{21}$$
$$= d_{11}^2 - 2d_{11}d_{22} + d_{22}^2 + 4d_{12}d_{21} = (d_{11} - d_{22})^2 + 4d_{12}^2 \geq 0$$

Thus no imaginary number can occur in r_1 and r_2.

(b) To have repeated roots, E has to be zero, which can occur if and only if $d_{11} = d_{22}$ (say, $= c$), and at the same time $d_{12} = d_{21} = 0$. This would mean that matrix D takes the form of $\begin{bmatrix} c & 0 \\ 0 & c \end{bmatrix}$.

(c) Positive or negative semidefiniteness requires at least one root to be zero, which is possible in the present case if and only if $E = (d_{11} + d_{22})^2$, that is, iff $d_{11}d_{22} - d_{12}d_{21} = 0$, or $|D| = 0$.

Exercise 11.4

1 The first-order condition

$$\begin{aligned} f_1 &= 2x_1 - 3x_2 &= 0 \\ f_2 &= -3x_1 + 6x_2 + 4x_3 &= 0 \\ f_3 &= 4x_2 + 12x_3 &= 0 \end{aligned}$$

is a homogeneous linear-equation system in which the three equations are independent. Thus the only solution is

$$\bar{x}_1 = \bar{x}_2 = \bar{x}_3 = 0 \qquad \text{so that} \qquad \bar{z} = 0$$

The Hessian is $\begin{vmatrix} 2 & -3 & 0 \\ -3 & 6 & 4 \\ 0 & 4 & 12 \end{vmatrix}$, with $|H_1| = 2 > 0$, $|H_2| = 3 > 0$,

and $|H_3| = 4 > 0$. Consequently, $\bar{z} = 0$ is a minimum.

2 The first-order condition consists of the three equations

$$f_1 = -2x_1 = 0 \qquad f_2 = -2x_2 = 0 \qquad f_3 = -2x_3 = 0$$

Thus $\quad \bar{x}_1 = \bar{x}_2 = \bar{x}_3 = 0 \qquad$ so that $\bar{z} = 29$

The Hessian is $\begin{vmatrix} -2 & 0 & 0 \\ 0 & -2 & 0 \\ 0 & 0 & -2 \end{vmatrix}$, with $|H_1| = -2 < 0$, $|H_2| = 4 > 0$,

and $|H_3| = -8 < 0$. Consequently, $\bar{z} = 29$ is a maximum.

3 The three equations in the first-order condition are

$$\begin{aligned} 2x_1 \qquad + x_3 &= 0 \\ 2x_2 + x_3 &= 1 \\ x_1 + x_2 + 6x_3 &= 0 \end{aligned}$$

Thus $\quad \bar{x}_1 = \frac{1}{20} \qquad \bar{x}_2 = \frac{11}{20} \qquad \bar{x}_3 = -\frac{2}{20} \qquad$ so that $\bar{z} = -\frac{11}{40}$

Since the Hessian is $\begin{vmatrix} 2 & 0 & 1 \\ 0 & 2 & 1 \\ 1 & 1 & 6 \end{vmatrix}$, with $|H_1| = 2 > 0$, $|H_2| = 4 > 0$,

and $|H_3| = 20 > 0$, the $\bar{z}$ value is a minimum.

4 The first-order condition involves the three equations

$$f_x = e^x - 1 = 0, \quad f_y = e^y - 1 = 0, \quad f_w = 2we^{w^2} - 2e^w = 0$$

Thus $\quad \bar{x} = 0 \quad \bar{y} = 0 \quad \bar{w} = 1 \quad$ so that $\bar{z} = 2 - e$

The Hessian is $\begin{vmatrix} e^x & 0 & 0 \\ 0 & e^y & 0 \\ 0 & 0 & 2(1+2w^2)e^{w^2} - 2e^w \end{vmatrix} = \begin{vmatrix} 1 & 0 & 0 \\ 0 & 1 & 0 \\ 0 & 0 & 4e \end{vmatrix}$ when

evaluated at the stationary point, with all principal minors positive. Thus $\bar{z}$ is a minimum.

5 By the first-order condition, we have

$$f_x = 2e^{2x} - 2 = 0, \quad f_y = -e^{-y} + 1 = 0, \quad f_w = 2we^{w^2} - 2e^w = 0$$

Thus $\quad \bar{x} = 0 \quad \bar{y} = 0 \quad \bar{w} = 1 \quad$ so that $\bar{z} = 2 - e$

The Hessian is $\begin{vmatrix} 4 & 0 & 0 \\ 0 & 1 & 0 \\ 0 & 0 & 4e \end{vmatrix}$ when evaluated at the stationary point,

with all principal minors positive. Thus $\bar{z}$ is a minimum.

6 (a) Problems 2, 4 and 5 yield diagonal Hessian matrices. The diagonal elements are all negative for problem 2, and all positive for problems 4 and 5.

(b) According to (11.16), these diagonal elements represent the characteristic roots. Thus the characteristic roots are all negative (d^2z negative definite) for problem 2, and all positive (d^2z positive definite) for problems 4 and 5.

(c) Yes.

7 (a) The characteristic equation is, by (11.14):

$$\begin{vmatrix} 2-r & 0 & 1 \\ 0 & 2-r & 1 \\ 1 & 1 & 6-r \end{vmatrix} = 0$$

Expanding the determinant by the method of Fig. 5.1, we get

$$(2 - r)(2 - r)(6 - r) - (2 - r) - (2 - r) = 0$$

or $(2 - r)[(2 - r)(6 - r) - 2] = 0$ [factoring]

or $(2 - r)(r^2 - 8r + 10) = 0$

Thus, from the $(2 - r)$ term, we have $r_1 = 2$. By the quadratic formula, we get from the other term: $r_2, r_3 = 4 \pm \sqrt{6}$.

(b) All three roots are positive. Thus d^2z is positive definite, and $\bar{z}$ is a minimum.

(c) Yes.

<u>Exercise 11.5</u>

1 (a) Let u and v be any two distinct points in the domain. Then

$$f(u) = u^2 \qquad f(v) = v^2 \qquad f[\theta u + (1 - \theta)v] = [\theta u + (1 - \theta)v]^2$$

Substituting these into (11.20), we find the difference between the left- and right-side expressions in (11.20) to be

$$\theta u^2 + (1 - \theta)v^2 - \theta^2u^2 - 2\theta(1 - \theta)\, uv - (1 - \theta)^2v^2$$

$$= \theta(1 - \theta)u^2 - 2\theta(1 - \theta)uv + \theta(1 - \theta)v^2$$

$$= \theta(1 - \theta)(u - v)^2 > 0 \qquad [\text{since } u \neq v]$$

Thus $z = x^2$ is a strictly convex function.

(b) Let $u = (u_1, u_2)$ and $v = (v_1, v_2)$ be any two distinct points in the domain. Then

$$f(u) = u_1^2 + 2u_2^2 \qquad f(v) = v_1^2 + 2v_2^2$$

$$f[\theta u + (1 - \theta)v] = [\theta u_1 + (1 - \theta)v_1]^2 + 2[\theta u_2 + (1 - \theta)v_2]^2$$

The difference between the left- and right-side expressions in (11.20) is

$$\theta(1 - \theta)(u_1^2 - 2u_1v_1 + v_1^2 + 2u_2^2 - 4u_2v_2 + 2v_2^2)$$

$$= \theta(1 - \theta)[(u_1 - v_1)^2 + 2(u_2 - v_2)^2] > 0$$

Thus $z = x_1^2 + 2x_2^2$ is a strictly convex function.

(c) Let $u = (u_1, u_2)$ and $v = (v_1, v_2)$ be any two distinct points in the domain. Then

$$f(u) = 2u_1^2 - u_1u_2 + u_2^2 \qquad f(v) = 2v_1^2 - v_1v_2 + v_2^2$$

$$f[\theta u + (1-\theta)v] = 2[\theta u_1 + (1-\theta)v_1]^2 - [\theta u_1 + (1-\theta)v_1]$$
$$\cdot[\theta u_2 + (1-\theta)v_2] + [\theta u_2 + (1-\theta)v_2]^2$$

The difference between the left- and right-side expressions in (11.20) is

$$\theta(1-\theta)[(2u_1^2 - 4u_1v_1 + 2v_1^2) - u_1u_2 + u_1v_2 + v_1u_2 - v_1v_2$$
$$+ (u_2^2 - 2u_2v_2 + v_2^2)]$$

$$= \theta(1-\theta)[2(u_1 - v_1)^2 - (u_1 - v_1)(u_2 - v_2) + (u_2 - v_2)^2] > 0$$

because the bracketed expression is positive, like $\theta(1-\theta)$. [The bracketed expression, a positive-definite quadratic form in the two variables $(u_1 - v_1)$ and $(u_2 - v_2)$, is positive since $(u_1 - v_1)$ and $(u_2 - v_2)$ are not both zero in our problem.] Thus $z = 2x^2 - xy + y^2$ is a strictly convex function.

2 (a) With $f'(u) = -2u$, the difference between the left- and right-side expressions in (11.24) is

$$-v^2 + u^2 + 2u(v - u) = -v^2 + 2uv - u^2 = -(v - u)^2 < 0$$

Thus $z = -x^2$ is strictly concave.

(b) Since $f_1(u_1, u_2) = f_2(u_1, u_2) = 2(u_1 + u_2)$, the difference between the left- and right-side expressions in (11.24') is

$$(v_1 + v_2)^2 - (u_1 + u_2)^2 - 2(u_1 + u_2)[(v_1 - u_1) + (v_2 - u_2)]$$
$$= (v_1 + v_2)^2 - 2(v_1 + v_2)(u_1 + u_2) + (u_1 + u_2)^2$$
$$= [(v_1 + v_2) - (u_1 + u_2)]^2 \geq 0$$

A zero value cannot be ruled out because the two points may be, e.g., $(u_1, u_2) = (5, 3)$ and $(v_1, v_2) = (2, 6)$. Thus $z = (x_1 + x_2)^2$ is convex, but not strictly so.

(c) Since $f_1(u_1, u_2) = -u_2$, and $f_2(u_1, u_2) = -u_1$, the difference between the left- and right-side expressions in (11.24') is

$$-v_1v_2 + u_1u_2 + u_2(v_1 - u_1) + u_1(v_2 - u_2)$$

$$= -v_1v_2 + v_1u_2 + u_1v_2 - u_1u_2 = (v_1 - u_1)(v_2 - u_2) \gtreqless 0$$

Thus $z = -xy$ is neither convex nor concave.

3 No. That theorem gives a sufficient condition which is not satisfied.

4 (a) No. (b) No. (c) Yes.

5 (a) The circle with its interior, i.e. a disk. (b) Yes.

6 (a) The set of points on an exponential curve; not a convex set.

(b) The set of points lying on or above an exponential curve; a convex set.

(c) The set of points lying on or below an inverse U-shaped curve; a convex set.

(d) The set of points lying on or above a rectangular hyperbola in the positive quadrant; a convex set.

7 (a) This is a convex combination, with $\theta = 0.5$.

(b) This is again a convex combination, with $\theta = 0.2$.

(c) This is not a convex combination.

8 (a) This set is the entire 2-space.

(b) This set is a cone bounded on one side by a ray passing through point u, and on the other side by a ray passing through point v.

(c) This set is the line segment uv.

9 (a) $S^{\leq} \equiv \{(x_1, \ldots, x_n) \mid f(x_1, \ldots, x_n) \leq k\}$ (f convex)

$S^{\geq} \equiv \{(x_1, \ldots, x_n) \mid g(x_1, \ldots, x_n) \geq k\}$ (g concave)

(b) $S^{\leq}$ is a solid circle (or disk); $S^{\geq}$ is a solid square.

Exercise 11.6

1 (a) No, because the marginal cost of one commodity will be independent of the output of the other.

(b) The first-order condition is

$$\pi_1 = P_{10} - 4Q_1 = 0 \qquad\qquad \pi_2 = P_{20} - 4Q_2 = 0$$

Thus $\overline{Q}_1 = \frac{1}{4} P_{10}$ and $\overline{Q}_2 = \frac{1}{4} P_{20}$. The profit is maximized, because the Hessian is $\begin{vmatrix} -4 & 0 \\ 0 & -4 \end{vmatrix}$, with $|H_1| < 0$ and $|H_2| > 0$. The signs of the principal minors do not depend on where they are evaluated. Thus the maximum in this problem is a unique absolute maximum.

(c) $\pi_{12} = 0$ implies that the profit-maximizing output level of one commodity is independent of the output of the other (see first-order condition). The firm can operate as if it has two plants, each optimizing the output of a different product.

2 (a) By the procedure used in Example 2 (taking Q_1 and Q_2 as choice variables), we can find

$$\overline{Q}_1 = 3\tfrac{4}{7} \qquad \overline{Q}_2 = 4\tfrac{9}{14} \qquad \overline{P}_1 = 6\tfrac{1}{14} \qquad \overline{P}_2 = 24\tfrac{2}{7}$$

(b) The Hessian is $\begin{vmatrix} -4 & 2 \\ 2 & -8 \end{vmatrix}$, with $|H_1| = -4$ and $|H_2| = 28$. Thus the sufficient condition for a maximum is met.

(c) Substituting the $\overline{P}$'s and $\overline{Q}$'s into the R and C functions, we get

$$\overline{R} = 134\tfrac{43}{98} \qquad \overline{C} = 65\tfrac{85}{98} \qquad \text{and} \qquad \overline{\pi} = 68\tfrac{4}{7}$$

3 $|\varepsilon_{d1}| = \left|\frac{dQ_1}{dP_1}\frac{\overline{P}_1}{\overline{Q}_1}\right| = \frac{1}{4}\frac{39}{6} = \frac{13}{8}$. Similarly, $|\varepsilon_{d2}| = \frac{1}{5}\frac{60}{9} = \frac{4}{3}$, and $|\varepsilon_{d3}| = \frac{1}{6}\frac{45}{5} = \frac{3}{2}$. The highest is $|\varepsilon_{d1}|$; the lowest is $|\varepsilon_{d2}|$.

4 (a) $C' = 15 + 2Q = 15 + 2Q_1 + 2Q_2 + 2Q_3$

(b) Equating each MR to the MC, we obtain the three equations:

$$10Q_1 + 2Q_2 + 2Q_3 = 45, \quad 2Q_1 + 12Q_2 + 2Q_3 = 90$$

$$\text{and} \quad 2Q_1 + 2Q_2 + 14Q_3 = 60$$

Thus $\overline{Q}_1 = 2\frac{88}{97}$, $\overline{Q}_2 = 6\frac{51}{97}$, $\overline{Q}_3 = 2\frac{91}{97}$.

(c) Substituting the above into the demand equations, we get

$$\bar{P}_1 = 51\tfrac{36}{97}, \qquad \bar{P}_2 = 72\tfrac{36}{97}, \qquad \bar{P}_3 = 57\tfrac{36}{97}$$

(d) Since $R_1'' = -8$, $R_2'' = -10$, $R_3'' = -12$, and $C'' = 2$, we do find that: (1) $R_1'' - C'' = -10 < 0$, (2) $R_1''R_2'' - (R_1'' + R_2'')C'' = 80 + 36 = 116 > 0$, and (3) $|H| = -960 - (80 + 96 + 120)(2) = -1552 < 0$.

5 (a) $\pi = P_0Q(a, b)(1 + \frac{1}{2}i_0)^{-2} - aP_{a0} - bP_{b0}$

(b) $\pi = P_0Q(a, b)(1 + \frac{1}{4}i_0)^{-3} - aP_{a0} - bP_{b0}$

6 $Q(a, b) = 260$

Exercise 11.7

1 (a) We may take (11.45) as the point of departure. Letting P_{a0} alone vary (i.e., letting $dP_0 = dP_{b0} = dr = dt = 0$), and dividing through by $dP_{a0} \neq 0$, we get the matrix equation

$$\begin{bmatrix} P_0Q_{aa}e^{-rt} & P_0Q_{ab}e^{-rt} \\ P_0Q_{ab}e^{-rt} & P_0Q_{bb}e^{-rt} \end{bmatrix} \begin{bmatrix} (\partial\bar{a}/\partial P_{a0}) \\ (\partial\bar{b}/\partial P_{a0}) \end{bmatrix} = \begin{bmatrix} 1 \\ 0 \end{bmatrix}$$

Hence, by Cramer's rule,

$$\left(\frac{\partial\bar{a}}{\partial P_{a0}}\right) = \frac{P_0Q_{bb}e^{-rt}}{|J|} < 0 \qquad \text{and} \qquad \left(\frac{\partial\bar{b}}{\partial P_{a0}}\right) = -\frac{P_0Q_{ab}e^{-rt}}{|J|} < 0$$

The higher the price of input a, the smaller will be the equilibrium levels of inputs a and b.

(b) Next, letting P_{b0} alone vary in (11.45), and dividing through by $dP_{b0} \neq 0$, we can obtain results similar to (a) above:

$$\left(\frac{\partial\bar{a}}{\partial P_{b0}}\right) = -\frac{P_0Q_{ab}e^{-rt}}{|J|} < 0 \qquad \text{and} \qquad \left(\frac{\partial\bar{b}}{\partial P_{b0}}\right) = \frac{P_0Q_{aa}e^{-rt}}{|J|} < 0$$

2 (a) P_0, i_0, P_{a0}, P_{b0}.

(b) From the first-order condition, we can check the Jacobian

$$|J| = \begin{vmatrix} \partial F^1/\partial a & \partial F^1/\partial b \\ \partial F^2/\partial a & \partial F^2/\partial b \end{vmatrix} = \begin{vmatrix} P_0Q_{aa}(1 + i_0)^{-1} & P_0Q_{ab}(1 + i_0)^{-1} \\ P_0Q_{ab}(1 + i_0)^{-1} & P_0Q_{bb}(1 + i_0)^{-1} \end{vmatrix}$$

$$= P_0^{2}(1 + i_0)^{-2}\begin{vmatrix} Q_{aa} & Q_{ab} \\ Q_{ab} & Q_{bb} \end{vmatrix}$$

to be positive at the initial equilibrium (optimum) since the second-order sufficient condition is assumed to be satisfied. By the implicit-function theorem, we can then write

$$\bar{a} = \bar{a}(P_0, i_0, P_{a0}, P_{b0}) \quad \text{and} \quad \bar{b} = \bar{b}(P_0, i_0, P_{a0}, P_{b0})$$

We can also write the identities

$$P_0Q_a(\bar{a}, \bar{b})(1 + i_0)^{-1} - P_{a0} \equiv 0$$

$$P_0Q_b(\bar{a}, \bar{b})(1 + i_0)^{-1} - P_{b0} \equiv 0$$

Taking total differentials, we get (after rearrangement) the following pair of equations corresponding to (11.45):

$$P_0Q_{aa}(1 + i_0)^{-1}\,d\bar{a} + P_0Q_{ab}(1 + i_0)^{-1}\,d\bar{b}$$

$$= -Q_a(1 + i_0)^{-1}\,dP_0 + P_0Q_a(1 + i_0)^{-2}\,di_0 + dP_{a0}$$

$$P_0Q_{ab}(1 + i_0)^{-1}\,d\bar{a} + P_0Q_{bb}(1 + i_0)^{-1}\,d\bar{b}$$

$$= -Q_b(1 + i_0)^{-1}\,dP_0 + P_0Q_b(1 + i_0)^{-2}\,di_0 + dP_{b0}$$

Letting P_0 alone vary (i.e., letting $d_{i0} = dP_{a0} = dP_{b0} = 0$), and dividing through by $dP_0 \neq 0$, we get

$$\begin{bmatrix} P_0Q_{aa}(1 + i_0)^{-1} & P_0Q_{ab}(1 + i_0)^{-1} \\ P_0Q_{ab}(1 + i_0)^{-1} & P_0Q_{bb}(1 + i_0)^{-1} \end{bmatrix}\begin{bmatrix} (\partial\bar{a}/\partial P_0) \\ (\partial\bar{b}/\partial P_0) \end{bmatrix} = \begin{bmatrix} -Q_a(1 + i_0)^{-1} \\ -Q_b(1 + i_0)^{-1} \end{bmatrix}$$

Thus $$\left(\frac{\partial\bar{a}}{\partial P_0}\right) = \frac{(Q_bQ_{ab} - Q_aQ_{bb})P_0(1 + i_0)^{-2}}{|J|} > 0$$

$$\left(\frac{\partial\bar{b}}{\partial P_0}\right) = \frac{(Q_aQ_{ab} - Q_bQ_{aa})P_0(1 + i_0)^{-2}}{|J|} > 0$$

(c) Letting i_0 alone vary, we can similarly obtain

$$\begin{bmatrix} P_0Q_{aa}(1 + i_0)^{-1} & P_0Q_{ab}(1 + i_0)^{-1} \\ P_0Q_{ab}(1 + i_0)^{-1} & P_0Q_{bb}(1 + i_0)^{-1} \end{bmatrix}\begin{bmatrix} (\partial\bar{a}/\partial i_0) \\ (\partial\bar{b}/\partial i_0) \end{bmatrix} = \begin{bmatrix} P_0Q_a(1 + i_0)^{-2} \\ P_0Q_b(1 + i_0)^{-2} \end{bmatrix}$$

Thus $$\left(\frac{\partial\bar{a}}{\partial i_0}\right) = \frac{(Q_aQ_{bb} - Q_bQ_{ab})P_0^{2}(1 + i_0)^{-3}}{|J|} < 0$$

$$\left(\frac{\partial \bar{b}}{\partial i_0}\right) = \frac{(Q_b Q_{aa} - Q_a Q_{ab}) P_0^2 (1 + i_0)^{-3}}{|J|} < 0$$

3 Differentiating (11.44) totally with respect to P_0, we get

$$Q_a e^{-rt} + P_0 Q_{aa}\left(\frac{\partial \bar{a}}{\partial P_0}\right) e^{-rt} + P_0 Q_{ab}\left(\frac{\partial \bar{b}}{\partial P_0}\right) e^{-rt} = 0$$

$$Q_b e^{-rt} + P_0 Q_{ab}\left(\frac{\partial \bar{a}}{\partial P_0}\right) e^{-rt} + P_0 Q_{bb}\left(\frac{\partial \bar{b}}{\partial P_0}\right) e^{-rt} = 0$$

Or, in matrix notation,

$$\begin{bmatrix} P_0 Q_{aa} e^{-rt} & P_0 Q_{ab} e^{-rt} \\ P_0 Q_{ab} e^{-rt} & P_0 Q_{bb} e^{-rt} \end{bmatrix} \begin{bmatrix} (\partial \bar{a}/\partial P_0) \\ (\partial \bar{b}/\partial P_0) \end{bmatrix} = \begin{bmatrix} -Q_a e^{-rt} \\ -Q_b e^{-rt} \end{bmatrix}$$

which leads directly to the results in (11.46).

4 In (11.42), the elements of the Jacobian determinant are first-order partial derivatives of the components of the first-order condition shown in (11.41). Thus, those elements are really the <u>second</u>-order partial derivatives of the (primitive) objective function -- exactly what are used to construct the Hessian determinant.

CHAPTER 12

Exercise 12.2

1 (a) $Z = xy + \lambda(2 - x - 2y)$. The necessary condition is:

$Z_\lambda = 2 - x - 2y = 0 \qquad Z_x = y - \lambda = 0 \qquad Z_y = x - 2\lambda = 0$

Thus $\bar{\lambda} = \frac{1}{2}$, $\bar{x} = 1$, $\bar{y} = \frac{1}{2}$ -- yielding $\bar{z} = \frac{1}{2}$.

(b) $Z = xy + 4x + \lambda(8 - x - y)$. The necessary condition is:

$Z_\lambda = 8 - x - y = 0 \qquad Z_x = y + 4 - \lambda = 0 \qquad Z_y = x - \lambda = 0$

Thus $\bar{\lambda} = 6$, $\bar{x} = 6$, $\bar{y} = 2$ -- yielding $\bar{z} = 36$.

(c) $Z = x - 3y - xy + \lambda(6 - x - y)$. The necessary condition is:

$Z_\lambda = 6 - x - y = 0 \qquad Z_x = 1 - y - \lambda = 0 \qquad Z_y = -3 - x - \lambda = 0$

Thus $\bar{\lambda} = -4$, $\bar{x} = 1$, $\bar{y} = 5$ -- yielding $\bar{z} = -19$.

(d) $Z = 7 - y + x^2 + \lambda(-x - y)$. The necessary condition is:

$Z_\lambda = -x - y = 0 \qquad Z_x = 2x - \lambda = 0 \qquad Z_y = -1 - \lambda = 0$

Thus $\bar{\lambda} = -1$, $\bar{x} = -\frac{1}{2}$, $\bar{y} = \frac{1}{2}$ -- yielding $\bar{z} = 6\frac{3}{4}$.

2 (a) Increase; at the rate $d\bar{z}/dc = \bar{\lambda} = 1/2$.

(b) Increase; $d\bar{z}/dc = 6$. (c) Decrease; $d\bar{z}/dc = 4$

(d) Decrease; $d\bar{z}/dc = -1$

3 (a) $Z = x + 2y + 3w + xy - yw + \lambda(10 - x - y - 2w)$. Hence:

$Z_\lambda = 10 - x - y - 2w = 0 \qquad Z_x = 1 + y - \lambda = 0$

$Z_y = 2 + x - w - \lambda = 0 \qquad Z_w = 3 - y - 2\lambda = 0$

(b) $Z = x^2 + 2xy + yw^2 + \lambda(24 - 2x - y - w^2) + \mu(8 - x - w)$. Thus

$Z_\lambda = 24 - 2x - y - w^2 = 0 \qquad Z_\mu = 8 - x - w = 0$

$Z_x = 2x + 2y - 2\lambda - \mu = 0 \qquad Z_y = 2x + w^2 - \lambda = 0$

$Z_w = 2yw + 2\lambda w - \mu = 0$

4 $Z = f(x, y) + \lambda[0 - G(x, y)] = f(x, y) - \lambda G(x, y)$. The first-order condition becomes:

$Z_\lambda = -G(x, y) = 0 \qquad Z_x = f_x - \lambda G_x = 0 \qquad Z_y = f_y - \lambda G_y = 0$

5 Since the constraint $g = c$ is to prevail at all times in this

constrained optimization problem, the equation takes on the sense of an identity, and it follows that dg must be zero. Then it follows that d^2g must be zero, too. In contrast, the equation $dz = 0$ is in the nature of a first-order condition--dz is not identically zero, but is being set equal to zero to locate the critical values of the choice variables. Thus d^2z does not have to be zero as a matter of course.

6 No, the sign of $\bar{\lambda}$ will be changed. The new $\bar{\lambda}$ is the negative of the old $\bar{\lambda}$.

<u>Exercise 12.3</u>

1 (a) Since $|\bar{H}| = \begin{vmatrix} 0 & 1 & 2 \\ 1 & 0 & 1 \\ 2 & 1 & 0 \end{vmatrix} = 4$, $\bar{z} = \frac{1}{2}$ is a maximum.

(b) Since $|\bar{H}| = \begin{vmatrix} 0 & 1 & 1 \\ 1 & 0 & 1 \\ 1 & 1 & 0 \end{vmatrix} = 2$, $\bar{z} = 36$ is a maximum.

(c) Since $|\bar{H}| = \begin{vmatrix} 0 & 1 & 1 \\ 1 & 0 & -1 \\ 1 & -1 & 0 \end{vmatrix} = -2$, $\bar{z} = -19$ is a minimum.

(d) Since $|\bar{H}| = \begin{vmatrix} 0 & 1 & 1 \\ 1 & 2 & 0 \\ 1 & 0 & -1 \end{vmatrix} = -1$, $\bar{z} = 6\frac{3}{4}$ is a minimum.

2 $|\bar{H}_1| = \begin{vmatrix} 0 & g_1 \\ g_1 & Z_{11} \end{vmatrix} = -g_1^2 < 0$

3 The zero can be made the last (instead of the first) element in the principal diagonal, with g_1, g_2 and g_3 (in that order) appearing in the last column and in the last row.

4 $|\bar{H}| = \begin{vmatrix} 0 & 0 & g_1^1 & g_2^1 & g_3^1 & g_4^1 \\ 0 & 0 & g_1^2 & g_2^2 & g_3^2 & g_4^2 \\ g_1^1 & g_1^2 & Z_{11} & Z_{12} & Z_{13} & Z_{14} \\ g_2^1 & g_2^2 & Z_{21} & Z_{22} & Z_{23} & Z_{24} \\ g_3^1 & g_3^2 & Z_{31} & Z_{32} & Z_{33} & Z_{34} \\ g_4^1 & g_4^2 & Z_{41} & Z_{42} & Z_{43} & Z_{44} \end{vmatrix}$

A sufficient condition for maximum z is: $|\bar{H}_3| < 0$ and $|\bar{H}_4| = |\bar{H}| > 0$.

A sufficient condition for minimum z is: $|\bar{H}_3| > 0$ and $|\bar{H}| > 0$.

Exercise 12.4

1 Examples of acceptable curves are:

(a) 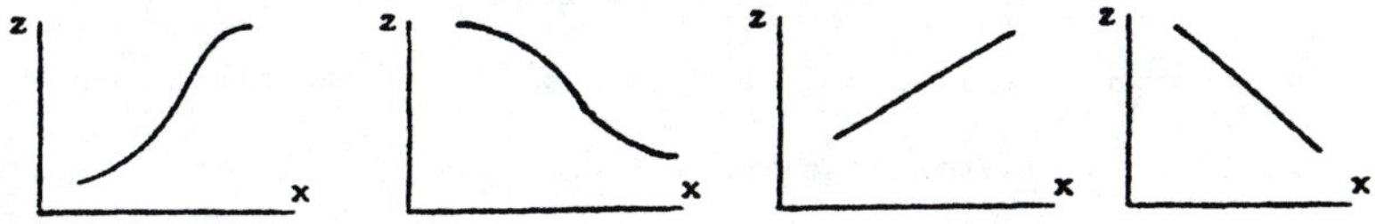

(b) 

(c) 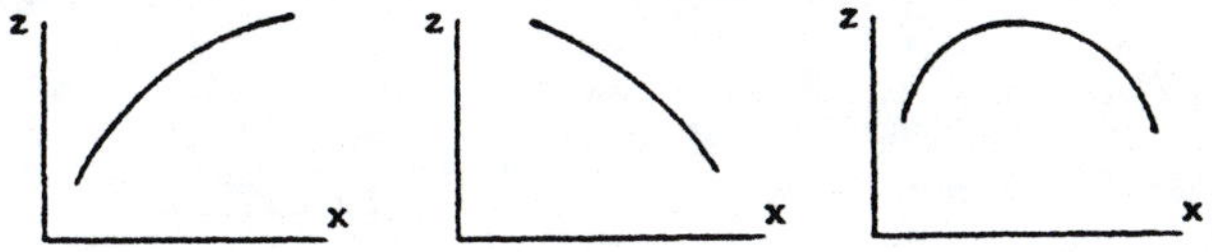

(d) 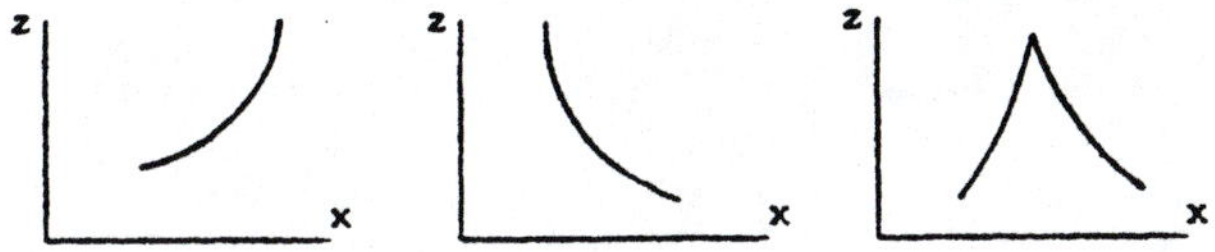

(e) 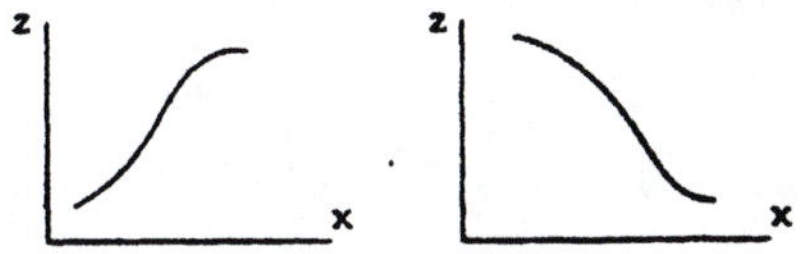

(f) 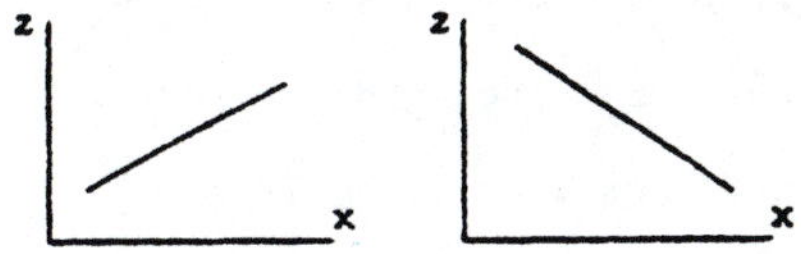

2 (a) 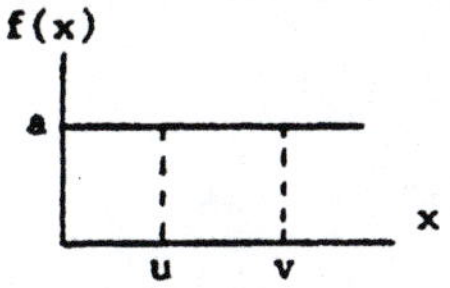

Quasiconcave, but not strictly so. This is because $f(v) = f(u) = a$, and thus $f[\theta u + (1 - \theta)v] = a$, which is equal to (not greater than) $f(u)$.

(b) 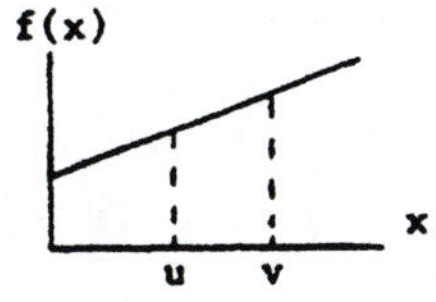

Quasiconcave, and strictly so. In the present case, $f(v) \geq f(u)$ means that $a + bv \geq a + bu$, or $v \geq u$. Moreover, to have u and v distinct, we must actually have $v > u$. Since

$$f[\theta u + (1 - \theta)v] = a + b[\theta u + (1 - \theta)v] = a + b[\theta u + (1 - \theta)v]$$

$$+ \underline{(bu - bu)} = a + bu + b(1 - \theta)(v - u) = f(u) + b(1 - \theta)(v - u)$$

$$= f(u) + \text{some positive term}$$

it follows that $f[\theta u + (1 - \theta)v] > f(u)$. Hence $f(x) = a + bx$, $(b > 0)$, is strictly quasiconcave.

(c)

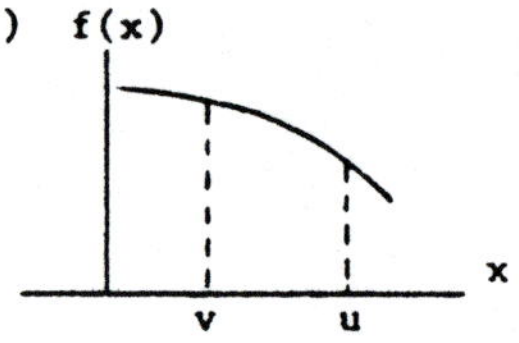

Quasiconcave, and strictly so. Here, $f(v) \geq f(u)$ means $a + cv^2 \geq a + cu^2$, or $v^2 \leq u^2$ (since $c < 0$). For nonnegative distinct values of u and v, this in turn means $v < u$. Now we have

$$f[\theta u + (1 - \theta)v] = a + c[\theta u + (1 - \theta)v]^2 + \underline{(cu^2 - cu^2)}$$

$$= a + cu^2 + c\{[\theta u + (1 - \theta)v]^2 - u^2\}$$

Using the identity $y^2 - x^2 \equiv (y + x)(y - x)$, we can rewrite the above expression as

$$a + cu^2 + c[\theta u + (1 - \theta)v + u][\theta u + (1 - \theta)v - u]$$

$$= f(u) + c[(1 + \theta)u + (1 - \theta)v][(1 - \theta)(v - u)]$$

$$= f(u) + \text{some positive term} > f(u)$$

Hence $f(x) = a + cx^2$, $(c < 0)$, is strictly quasiconcave.

3 Both $f(x)$ and $g(x)$ are monotonic, and thus quasiconcave. However, $f(x) + g(x)$ displays both a hill and a valley. If we pick $k = 5\frac{1}{2}$, for instance, neither $S^{\geq}$ nor $S^{\leq}$ will be a convex set. Therefore $f(x) + g(x)$ is not quasiconcave.

4 (a) This cubic function has a graph similar to Fig. 2.8c, with a hill in the second quadrant and valley in the fourth. If we pick $k = 0$, neither $S^{\geq}$ nor $S^{\leq}$ is a convex set. The function is neither quasiconcave nor quasiconvex.

(b) This function is linear, and hence both quasiconcave and quasiconvex.

(c) Setting $x_2 - \ln x_1 = k$, and solving for x_2, we get the isovalue equation $x_2 = \ln x_1 + k$. In the x_1x_2 plane, this plots for each value of k as a log curve shifted upward vertically by the amount of k. The set $S^{\leq} = \{(x_1, x_2) \mid f(x_1, x_2) \leq k\}$ -- the set of points on or below the isovalue curve--is a convex set. Thus the function is quasiconvex (but not quasiconcave).

5 (a) A cubic curve contains two bends, and would thus violate both parts of (12.21).

(b) From the discussion of the cubic total-cost function in Sec. 9.4, we know that if a, c, d > 0, b < 0, and $b^2 < 3ac$, then the cubic function will be upward-sloping for nonnegative x. Then, by (12.21), it is both quasiconcave and quasiconvex.

6 Let u and v be two values of x, and let $f(v) = v^2 \geq f(u) = u^2$, which implies $v \geq u$. Since $f'(x) = 2x$, we find that

$$f'(u)(v - u) = 2u(v - u) \geq 0$$

$$f'(v)(v - u) = 2v(v - u) \geq 0$$

Thus, by (12.22), the function is both quasiconcave and quasiconvex, confirming the conclusion in Example 1.

7 The set $S^{\leq}$, involving the inequality $xy \leq k$, consists of t.. points lying on or below a rectangular hyperbola--not a convex set. Hence the function is quasiconvex by (12.21). Alternatively, since $f_x = y$, $f_y = x$, $f_{xx} = 0$, $f_{xy} = 1$, and $f_{yy} = 0$, we have $|B_1| = -y^2 \leq 0$ and $|B_2| = 2xy \geq 0$, which violates the necessary condition (12.25') for quasiconvexity.

8 (a) Since $f_x = -2x$, $f_y = -2y$, $f_{xx} = -2$, $f_{xy} = 0$, $f_{yy} = -2$, we have

$$|B_1| = -4x^2 < 0 \qquad |B_2| = 8(x^2 + y^2) > 0$$

By (12.26), the funciton is quasiconcave.

(b) Since $f_x = -2(x + 1)$, $f_y = -2(y + 2)$, $f_{xx} = -2$, $f_{xy} = 0$,

$f_{yy} = -2$, we have

$|B_1| = -4(x + 1)^2 < 0$ $\qquad$ $|B_2| = 8(x + 1)^2 + 8(y + 2)^2 > 0$

By (12.26), the function is quasiconcave.

Exercise 12.5

1 (a) $Z = (x + 2)(y + 1) + \lambda(130 - 4x - 6y)$

(b) The first-order condition requires that

$Z_\lambda = 130 - 4x - 6y = 0, \quad Z_x = y + 1 - 4\lambda = 0, \quad Z_y = x + 2 - 6\lambda = 0$

Thus we have $\bar{\lambda} = 3$, $\bar{x} = 16$, and $\bar{y} = 11$.

(c) $|\bar{H}| = \begin{vmatrix} 0 & 4 & 6 \\ 4 & 0 & 1 \\ 6 & 1 & 0 \end{vmatrix} = 48 > 0$. Hence utility is maximized.

(d) No.

2 (a) $Z = (x + 2)(y + 1) + \lambda(B - xP_x - yP_y)$

(b) As the necessary condition for extremum, we have

$$\begin{aligned} Z_\lambda &= B - xP_x - yP_y = 0 & \text{or} \quad & -P_x x - P_y y = -B \\ Z_x &= y + 1 - \lambda P_x = 0 & & -P_x\lambda + y = -1 \\ Z_y &= x + 2 - \lambda P_y = 0 & & -P_y\lambda + x = -2 \end{aligned}$$

By Cramer's rule, we can find that

$$\bar{\lambda} = \frac{B + 2P_x + P_y}{2P_xP_y} \qquad \bar{x} = \frac{B - 2P_x + P_y}{2P_x} \qquad \bar{y} = \frac{B + 2P_x - P_y}{2P_y}$$

(c) $|\bar{H}| = \begin{vmatrix} 0 & P_x & P_y \\ P_x & 0 & 1 \\ P_y & 1 & 0 \end{vmatrix} = 2P_xP_y > 0$. Utility is maximized.

(d) When $P_x = 4$, $P_y = 6$, and $B = 130$, we get $\bar{\lambda} = 3$, $\bar{x} = 16$ and $\bar{y} = 11$. These check with the preceding problem.

3 Yes. $\left(\frac{\partial\bar{x}}{\partial B}\right) = \frac{1}{2P_x} > 0$, $\left(\frac{\partial\bar{x}}{\partial P_x}\right) = -\frac{B + P_y}{2P_x^2} < 0$, $\left(\frac{\partial\bar{x}}{\partial P_y}\right) = \frac{1}{2P_x} > 0$,

$\left(\frac{\partial\bar{y}}{\partial B}\right) = \frac{1}{2P_y} > 0$, $\left(\frac{\partial\bar{y}}{\partial P_x}\right) = \frac{1}{P_y} > 0$, $\left(\frac{\partial\bar{y}}{\partial P_y}\right) = -\frac{B + 2P_x}{2P_y^2} < 0$.

An increase in income B raises the level of optimal purchases of x and y both; an increase in the price of one commodity reduces the optimal purchase of that commodity itself, but raises the optimal purchase of the other commodity.

4 We have $U_{xx} = U_{yy} = 0$, $U_{xy} = U_{yx} = 1$, $|J| = |\overline{H}| = 2P_x P_y$. $\overline{x} = (B - 2P_x + P_y)/2P_x$, and $\overline{\lambda} = (B + 2P_x + P_y)/2P_x P_y$. Thus:

(a) $(\partial\overline{x}/\partial B) = 1/2P_x$, and $(\partial\overline{y}/\partial B) = 1/2P_y$.

(b) $(\partial\overline{x}/\partial P_x) = -(B + P_y)/2P_x^2$, and $(\partial\overline{y}/\partial P_x) = 1/p_y$.

These answers check with the preceding problem.

5 A negative sign for that derivative can mean <u>either</u> that the income effect (T_1) and the substitution effect (T_2) in (12.33') are both negative (normal good), <u>or</u> that the income effect is positive (inferior good) but is overshadowed by the negative substitution effect. The statement is not valid.

6 The optimal utility level can be expressed as $\overline{U} = \overline{U}(\overline{x}, \overline{y})$. Thus $d\overline{U} = U_x\, d\overline{x} + U_y\, d\overline{y}$, where U_x and U_y are evaluated at the optimum. When $\overline{U}$ is constant, we have $d\overline{U} = 0$, or $U_x\, d\overline{x} + U_y\, d\overline{y} = 0$. From (12.31"), we have $U_x/U_y = P_x/P_y$ at the optimum. Thus we can also express $d\overline{U} = 0$ by $P_x\, d\overline{x} + P_y\, d\overline{y} = 0$, or $-P_x\, d\overline{x} - P_y\, d\overline{y} = 0$.

7 (a) No; diminishing marginal utility means only that U_{xx} and U_{yy} are negative, but says nothing about U_{xy}. Therefore we cannot be sure that $|\overline{H}| > 0$ in (12.32) and $d^2y/dx^2 > 0$ in (12.33').

(b) No; if $d^2y/dx^2 > 0$, and hence $|\overline{H}| > 0$, nothing definite can be said about the sign of U_{xx} and U_{yy}, because U_{xy} also appears in $|\overline{H}|$.

<u>Exercise 12.6</u>

1 (a) $\sqrt{(jx)(jy)} = j\sqrt{xy}$; homogeneous of degree one.

(b) $[(jx)^2 - (jy)^2]^{1/2} = j(x^2 - y^2)^{1/2}$; homogeneous of degree one.

(c) Not homogeneous.

(d) $2jx + jy + 3\sqrt{(jx)(jy)} = j(2x + y + 3\sqrt{xy})$; homogeneous of degree one.

(e) $\frac{(jx)(jy)^2}{jw} + 2(jx)(jw) = j^2(\frac{xy^2}{w} + 2xw)$; homogeneous of degree two.

(f) $(jx)^4 - 5(jy)(jw)^3 = j^4(x^4 - 5yw^3)$; homogeneous of degree four.

2 Let $j = \frac{1}{K}$, then $\frac{Q}{K} = f(\frac{K}{K}, \frac{L}{K}) = f(1, \frac{L}{K}) = \psi(\frac{L}{K})$. Thus $Q = K\psi(\frac{L}{K})$.

3 (a) When $MPP_K = 0$, we have $L\frac{\partial Q}{\partial L} = Q$, or $\frac{\partial Q}{\partial L} = \frac{Q}{L}$, or $MPP_L = APP_L$.

(b) When $MPP_L = 0$, we have $K\frac{\partial Q}{\partial K} = Q$, or $\frac{\partial Q}{\partial K} = \frac{Q}{K}$, or $MPP_K = APP_K$.

4 Yes, they are true:

(a) $APP_L = \phi(k)$; hence APP_L indeed can be plotted against k.

(b) $MPP_K = \phi'(k) =$ slope of APP_L.

(c) $APP_K = \frac{\phi(k)}{k} = \frac{APP_L}{k} = \frac{\text{ordinate of a point on the } APP_L \text{ curve}}{\text{abscissa of that point}}$

$=$ slope of radius vector to the APP_L curve

(d) $MPP_L = \phi(k) - k\phi'(k) = APP_L - k \cdot MPP_K$.

5 (b) $APP_L = Ak^\alpha$, thus the slope of $APP_L = A\alpha k^{\alpha-1} = MPP_K$.

(c) Slope of a radius vector $= Ak^\alpha/k = Ak^{\alpha-1} = APP_K$.

(d) $APP_L - k \cdot MPP_K = Ak^\alpha - kA\alpha k^{\alpha-1} = Ak^\alpha - A\alpha k^\alpha = A(1 - \alpha)k^\alpha = MPP_L$.

6 (a) Since the function is homogeneous of degree $(\alpha + \beta)$, if $\alpha + \beta > 1$, the value of the function will increase more than j-fold when K and L are increased j-fold, implying increasing returns to scale.

(b) If $\alpha + \beta < 1$, the value of the function will increase less than j-fold when K and L are increased j-fold, implying decreasing returns to scale.

(c) Taking the natural log of both sides of the function, we have

$$\ln Q = \ln A + \alpha \ln K + \beta \ln L$$

Thus $\epsilon_{QK} = \frac{\partial(\ln Q)}{\partial(\ln K)} = \alpha$ and $\epsilon_{QL} = \frac{\partial(\ln Q)}{\partial(\ln L)} = \beta$

7 (a) $A(jK)^a(jL)^b(jN)^c = j^{a+b+c} \cdot AK^aL^bN^c = j^{a+b+c}\ Q$; homogeneous of degree $a + b + c$.

(b) $a + b + c = 1$ implies constant returns to scale; $a + b + c > 1$ implies increasing returns to scale.

(c) Share for $N = \frac{N(\partial Q/\partial N)}{Q} = \frac{NAK^aL^bcN^{c-1}}{AK^aL^bN^c} = c$

8 (a) $j^2Q = g(jK, jL)$

(b) Let $j = 1/L$. Then the euqation in (a) yields:

$Q/L^2 = g(K/L, 1) = \phi(K/L) = \phi(k)$. This implies that $Q = L^2\phi(k)$.

(c) $MPP_K = \partial Q/\partial K = L^2\phi'(k)(\partial k/\partial K) = L^2\phi'(k)(1/L) = L\phi'(k)$. Now MPP_K depends on L as well as k.

(d) If K and L are both increased j-fold in the MPP_K expression in (c), we get

$$(jL)\phi'(\frac{jK}{jL}) = jL\phi'(\frac{K}{L}) = jL\phi'(k) = j \cdot MPP_K$$

Thus MPP_K is homogeneous of degree one in K and L.

Exercise 12.7

1 (a) Linear homogeneity implies that the output levels of the isoquants are in the ratio of 1:2:3 (from southwest to northeast).

(b) With second-degree homogeneity, the output levels are in the ratio of $1:2^2:3^2$, or 1:4:9.

2 Since $(\overline{b}/\overline{a}) = (\beta/\alpha)(P_a/P_b)$, it will plot as a straight line passing through the origin, with a (positive) slope equal to β/α. This result does not depend on the assumption $\alpha + \beta = 1$. The elasticity of substitution is merely the elasticity of this line, which can be read (by the method of Fig. 8.2) to be unity at all points.

3 Yes, because Q_{LL} and Q_{KK} have both been found to be negative.

4 On the basis of (12.66), we have

$$\frac{d^2K}{dL^2} = \frac{d}{dL}\left[\frac{\delta - 1}{\delta}\left(\frac{K}{L}\right)^{1+\rho}\right] = \frac{\delta - 1}{\delta}(1 + \rho)\left(\frac{K}{L}\right)^{\rho}\frac{d}{dL}\left(\frac{K}{L}\right)$$

$$= \frac{\delta - 1}{\delta}(1 + \rho)\left(\frac{K}{L}\right)^{\rho}\frac{1}{L^2}\left(L\frac{dK}{dL} - K\right) > 0 \qquad \left[\text{because } \frac{dK}{dL} < 0\right]$$

5 (a) $\dfrac{\text{Labor share}}{\text{Capital share}} = \dfrac{Lf_L}{Kf_K} = \dfrac{1 - \delta}{\delta}\left(\dfrac{K}{L}\right)^{\rho}$. A larger ρ implies a larger capital share in relation to the labor share.

(b) No; no.

6 (a) If $\rho = -1$, (12.66) yields $dK/dL = -(1 - \delta)/\delta$ = constant. The isoquants would be downward-sloping straight lines.

(b) By (12.68), σ is not defined for $\rho = -1$. But as $\rho \to -1$, $\sigma \to \infty$.

(c) Linear isoquants and infinite elasticity of substitution both imply that the two inputs are perfect substitutes.

7 If both K and L are changed j-fold, output will change from Q to:

$$A[\delta(jK)^{-\rho} + (1 - \delta)(jL)^{-\rho}]^{-r/\rho} = A\{j^{-\rho}[\delta K^{-\rho} + (1 - \delta)L^{-\rho}]\}^{-r/\rho}$$
$$= (j^{-\rho})^{-r/\rho}Q = j^{r}Q$$

Hence r denotes the degree of homogeneity. With $r > 1$ ($r < 1$), we have increasing (decreasing) returns to scale.

8 By L'Hôpital's rule, we have:

(a) $\displaystyle\lim_{x\to4}\frac{x^2 - x - 12}{x - 4} = \lim_{x\to4}\frac{2x - 1}{1} = 7$

(b) $\displaystyle\lim_{x\to0}\frac{e^x - 1}{x} = \lim_{x\to0}\frac{e^x}{1} = 1$

(c) $\displaystyle\lim_{x\to0}\frac{5^x - e^x}{x} = \lim_{x\to0}\frac{5^x \ln 5 - e^x}{1} = \ln 5 - 1$

(d) $\displaystyle\lim_{x\to\infty}\frac{\ln x}{x} = \lim_{x\to\infty}\frac{1/x}{1} = 0$

9 (a) By successive applications of the rule, we find that

$$\lim_{x\to\infty}\frac{x^n}{e^x} = \lim_{x\to\infty}\frac{nx^{n-1}}{e^x} = \lim_{x\to\infty}\frac{n(n - 1)x^{n-2}}{e^x} = \ldots = \lim_{x\to\infty}\frac{n!}{e^x} = 0$$

(b) By taking $m(x) = \ln x$, and $n(x) = \frac{1}{x}$, we have

$$\lim_{x\to0^+}\frac{\ln x}{1/x} = \lim_{x\to0^+}\frac{1/x}{-1/x^2} = \lim_{x\to0^+} -x = 0$$

(c) Since $x^x = \exp(\ln x^x) = \exp(x \ln x)$, and since, from (b) above, the expression $x \ln x$ tends to zero as $x \to 0^+$, x^x must tend to $e^0 = 1$ as $x \to 0^+$.

CHAPTER 13

Exercise 13.2

1 (a) $\int 16x^{-3}\,dx = 16\frac{x^{-2}}{-2} + c = -8x^{-2} + c \qquad (x \neq 0)$

(b) $\int 9x^8\,dx = x^9 + c$

(c) $\int x^5\,dx - 3\int x\,dx = \frac{1}{6}x^6 - \frac{3}{2}x^2 + c$

(d) If $f(x) = -2x$, then $f'(x) = -2$. Using Rule IIa, we have

$$-\int (-2)e^{-2x}\,dx = -\int f'(x)e^{f(x)}\,dx = -e^{f(x)} + c = -e^{-2x} + c$$

(e) If $f(x) = x^2 + 1$, then $f'(x) = 2x$. Using Rule IIIa, we have

$$2\int \frac{2x}{x^2+1}\,dx = 2\int \frac{f'(x)}{f(x)}\,dx = 2\ln f(x) + c = 2\ln(x^2+1) + c$$

(f) Let $u = ax^2 + bx$. Then $du/dx = 2ax + b$. Thus

$$\int \frac{du}{dx}u^7\,dx = \int u^7\,du = \frac{1}{8}u^8 + c = \frac{1}{8}(ax^2 + bx)^8 + c$$

2 (a) $13\int e^x\,dx = 13e^x + c$

(b) $3\int e^x\,dx + 4\int \frac{1}{x}\,dx = 3e^x + 4\ln x + c \qquad (x > 0)$

(c) $5\int e^x\,dx + 3\int x^{-2}\,dx = 5e^x - 3x^{-1} + c \qquad (x \neq 0)$

(d) Let $u = -(2x + 7)$. Then $du/dx = -2$. Thus

$$\int 3e^{-(2x+7)}\,dx = \int 3\left(-\frac{1}{2}\frac{du}{dx}\right)e^u\,dx = -\frac{3}{2}\int e^u\,du = -\frac{3}{2}e^u + c$$

$$= -\frac{3}{2}e^{-(2x+7)} + c$$

(e) Let $u = x^2 + 3$. Then $du/dx = 2x$, and

$$\int 4xe^{x^2+3}\,dx = \int 2\frac{du}{dx}e^u\,dx = 2\int e^u\,du = 2e^u + c = 2e^{x^2+3} + c$$

(f) Let $u = x^2 + 9$. Then $du/dx = 2x$, and

$$\int xe^{x^2+9}\,dx = \int \frac{1}{2}\frac{du}{dx}e^u\,dx = \frac{1}{2}\int e^u\,du = \frac{1}{2}e^u + c = \frac{1}{2}e^{x^2+9} + c$$

3(a) $\int \frac{3\,dx}{x} = 3\int \frac{dx}{x} = 3\ln|x| + c \qquad (x \neq 0)$

(b) Let $u = x - 2$. Then $du/dx = 1$, and

$$\int \frac{dx}{x-2} = \int \frac{1}{u}\frac{du}{dx}\,dx = \int \frac{1}{u}\,du = \ln|u| + c = \ln|x-2| + c$$

$(x \neq 2)$

(c) Let $u = x^2 + 3$. Then $du/dx = 2x$, and

$$\int \frac{du}{dx}\frac{1}{u}\,dx = \int \frac{du}{u} = \ln u + c = \ln (x^2 + 3) + c$$

(d) Let $u = 3x^2 + 5$. Then $du/dx = 6x$, and

$$\int (\frac{1}{6}\frac{du}{dx})\frac{1}{u}\,dx = \frac{1}{6}\int \frac{du}{u} = \frac{1}{6}\ln u + c = \frac{1}{6}\ln (3x^2 + 5) + c$$

4 (a) Let $v = x + 3$, and $u = \frac{2}{3}(x + 1)^{3/2}$, so that $dv = dx$ and $du = (x + 1)^{1/2}\,dx$. Then, by Rule VII, we have

$$\int (x + 3)(x + 1)^{1/2}\,dx = \frac{2}{3}(x + 1)^{3/2}(x + 3) - \int \frac{2}{3}(x + 1)^{3/2}\,dx$$
$$= \frac{2}{3}(x + 1)^{3/2}(x + 3) - \frac{4}{15}(x + 1)^{5/2} + c$$

(b) Let $v = \ln x$ and $u = \frac{1}{2}x^2$, so that $dv = \frac{1}{x}\,dx$ and $du = x\,dx$.

Then Rule VII gives us

$$\int x \ln x\,dx = \frac{1}{2}x^2 \ln x - \int \frac{1}{2}x^2\frac{1}{x}\,dx = \frac{1}{2}x^2 \ln x - \frac{1}{4}x^2 + c$$
$$= \frac{1}{4}x^2(2 \ln x - 1) + c \qquad (x > 0)$$

5 $$\int [k_1f_1(x) + \dots + k_nf_n(x)]\,dx = \int k_1f_1(x)\,dx + \dots + \int k_nf_n(x)\,dx$$
$$= k_1\int f_1(x)\,dx + \dots + k_n\int f_n(x)\,dx = \sum_{i=1}^{n} k_i \int f_i(x)\,dx$$

Exercise 13.3

1 (a) $\frac{1}{6}x^3\Big]_1^3 = \frac{1}{6}(3^3 - 1^3) = \frac{26}{6} = 4\frac{1}{3}$

(b) $\left[\frac{x^4}{4} + 3x^2\right]_0^1 = (\frac{1}{4} + 3) - 0 = 3\frac{1}{4}$

(c) $2x^{3/2}\Big]_1^3 = 2\sqrt{x^3}\,\Big]_1^3 = 2\sqrt{27} - 2$

(d) $\left[\frac{x^4}{4} - 2x^3\right]_2^4 = [\frac{4^4}{4} - 2(4)^3] - [\frac{2^4}{4} - 2(2)^3] = (64 - 128) - (4 - 16)$
$= -52$

(e) $\left[\frac{a}{3}x^3 + \frac{b}{2}x^2 + cx\right]_{-1}^{1} = (\frac{a}{3} + \frac{b}{2} + c) - (-\frac{a}{3} + \frac{b}{2} - c) = 2(\frac{a}{3} + c)$

(f) $\frac{1}{2}(\frac{x^3}{3} + 1)^2\Big]_4^2 = \frac{1}{2}[(\frac{8}{3} + 1)^2 - (\frac{64}{3} + 1)^2] = \frac{1}{2}\,\frac{121 - 4489}{9}$

$$= -\frac{4368}{18} = -242\frac{2}{3}$$

2 (a) $-\frac{1}{2}e^{-2x}\Big]_1^2 = -\frac{1}{2}(e^{-4} - e^{-2}) = \frac{1}{2}(e^{-2} - e^{-4})$

(b) $\ln|x+2|\Big]_{-1}^{e-2} = \ln e - \ln 1 = 1 - 0 = 1$

(c) $\left[\frac{1}{2}e^{2x} + e^{x}\right]_2^3 = (\frac{1}{2}e^6 + e^3) - (\frac{1}{2}e^4 + e^2)$

$$= e^2(\frac{1}{2}e^4 - \frac{1}{2}e^2 + e - 1)$$

(d) $\left[\ln|x| + \ln|1+x|\right]_e^6 = \left[\ln|x(1+x)|\right]_e^6$

$$= \ln 42 - \ln[e(1+e)] = \ln\frac{42}{e(1+e)}$$

3 (a) $A^{**} = \sum_{i=1}^{4} f(x_{i+1})\,\Delta x_i$ (b) $A^{**} < A$; underestimate.

(c) A^{**} would approach A. (d) Yes.

(e) $f(x)$ is Riemann integrable.

4 The curve refers to the graph of the integrand $f(x)$. If we plot the graph of $F(x)$, the definite integral--which has the value $F(b) - F(a)$--will show up there as a vertical distance.

5 (a) $\frac{c}{b}x\Big]_0^b = c - 0 = c$ (b) $t\Big]_0^c = c - 0 = c$

Exercise 13.4

1 None is improper.

2 (a) and (d) each has an infinite limit of integration: (c) and (e) have infinite integrands, at $x = 0$ and $x = 2$, respectively.

3 (a) $\int_0^\infty e^{-rt}\,dt = \lim_{b\to\infty}\int_0^b e^{-rt}\,dt = \lim_{b\to\infty}\left[-\frac{1}{r}e^{-rt}\right]_0^b$

$$= \lim_{b\to\infty} -\frac{1}{r}(e^{-rb} - e^0) = -\frac{1}{r}(0 - 1) = \frac{1}{r}$$

(c) $\int_0^1 x^{-2/3}\,dx = \lim_{a\to 0^+}\int_a^1 x^{-2/3}\,dx = \lim_{a\to 0^+}\left[3x^{1/3}\right]_a^1 = 3$

(d) $\int_{-\infty}^{0} e^{rt}\, dt = \lim_{a\to-\infty}\left[\frac{1}{r} e^{rt}\right]_a^0 = \frac{1}{r}(1 - 0) = \frac{1}{r}$

(e) $\int_1^5 \frac{dx}{x-2} = \int_1^2 \frac{dx}{x-2} + \int_2^5 \frac{dx}{x-2}$

$$= \lim_{b\to 2^-}\left[\ln|x-2|\right]_1^b + \lim_{a\to 2^+}\left[\ln(x-2)\right]_a^5 = I_1 + I_2$$

$I_1 = \lim_{b\to 2^-}[\ln|b-2| - \ln 1] = -\infty$; and $I_2 = \lim_{a\to 2^+}[\ln 3 - \ln(a-2)] = +\infty$.

This integral is divergent. (I_1 and I_2 cannot cancel each other out.)

4 $I_2 = \lim_{a\to 0^+}\int_a^1 x^{-3}\, dx = \lim_{a\to 0^+}\left[-\frac{1}{2}x^{-2}\right]_a^1 = \lim_{a\to 0^+}\left(-\frac{1}{2} + \frac{1}{2a^2}\right) = +\infty$

5 (a)

(b) Area $= \int_0^\infty ce^{-t}\, dt = \lim_{b\to\infty}\left[-ce^{-t}\right]_0^b = c$ (finite)

Exercise 13.5

1 (a) $R(Q) = \int (28Q - e^{0.3Q})\, dQ = 14Q^2 - \frac{10}{3}e^{0.3Q} + c$. The initial condition is $R(0) = 0$. Setting $Q = 0$ in $R(Q)$, we find $R(0) = -\frac{10}{3} + c$. Thus $c = \frac{10}{3}$. And $R(Q) = 14Q^2 - \frac{10}{3}e^{0.3Q} + \frac{10}{3}$.

(b) $R(Q) = \int 10(1+Q)^{-2}\, dQ$. Let $u = 1 + Q$. Then $du/dQ = 1$, or $du = dQ$, and $R(Q) = 10\int u^{-2}\, du = 10(-u^{-1}) + c = -10(1+Q)^{-1} + c$. Since $R(0) = 0$, we have $0 = -10 + c$, or $c = 10$. Thus

$$R(Q) = \frac{-10}{1+Q} + 10 = \frac{-10 + 10 + 10Q}{1+Q} = \frac{10Q}{1+Q}$$

2 (a) $M(Y) = \int 0.1\, dY = 0.1Y + c$. From the initial condition, we have $20 = 0.1(0) + c$, giving us $c = 20$. Thus $M(Y) = 0.1Y + 20$.

(b) $C(Y) = \int (0.8 + 0.1Y^{-1/2})\, dY = 0.8Y + 0.2Y^{1/2} + c$. From the side information, we have $100 = 0.8(100) + 0.2(100)^{1/2} + c$, or $c = 18$. Thus $C(Y) = 0.8Y + 0.2Y^{1/2} + 18$.

3 (a) $K(t) = \int 12t^{1/3}\,dt = 9t^{4/3} + c$. Since $K(0) = 25$, we have $25 = 9(0) + c$, so that $c = 25$. Thus $K(t) = 9t^{4/3} + 25$.

(b) $K(1) - K(0) = 9t^{4/3}\Big]_0^1 = 9$; $K(3) - K(1) = 9\Big[t^{4/3}\Big]_1^3$

$$= 9[3(3^{1/3}) - 1]$$

4 (a) $\Pi = \frac{1000}{0.05}[1 - e^{-0.05(2)}] = 20{,}000[1 - e^{-0.10}]$

$$= 20{,}000(0.0952) = 1904.00 \text{ (approximately)}$$

(b) $\Pi = \frac{1000}{0.04}[1 - e^{-0.04(3)}] = 25{,}000[1 - e^{-0.12}]$

$$= 25{,}000(0.1131) = 2827.50 \text{ (approximately)}$$

5 (a) $\Pi = \$1450/0.05 = \$29{,}000$ (b) $\Pi = \$2460/0.08 = \$30{,}750$

Exercise 13.6

1 Capital alone is considered. More specifically, the production function is $\kappa = \rho K$. The constancy of the capacity-capital ratio ρ means that the output level is a specific multiple of the amount of capital used. Since the production process obviously requires the labor factor as well, the equation above implies that labor and capital are combined in a fixed proportion, for only then can we consider capital alone to the exclusion of labor. This also seems to carry the implication of a perfectly elastic supply of labor.

2 The second equation in (13.16) states that the rate of growth of I is the constant ρs. Thus the investment function should be $I(t) = Ae^{\rho st}$, where A can be definitized to $I(0)$.

3 If $I < 0$, then $|I| = -I$. Thus the equation $|I| = Ae^{\rho st}$ becomes $-I = Ae^{\rho st}$. Setting $t = 0$, we find that $-I(0) = Ae^{0} = A$. Thus

we now have $-I = -I(0)e^{\rho st}$, which is identical with (13.18).

4 Left side $= \int_0^t \frac{1}{I}\frac{dI}{dt}\,dt = \int_{I(0)}^{I(t)} \frac{1}{I}\,dI = \ln I\Big]_{I(0)}^{I(t)}$

$$\ln I(t) - \ln I(0) = \ln \frac{I(t)}{I(0)}$$

Right side $= \int_0^t \rho s\,dt = \rho st\Big]_0^t = \rho st$

Equating the two sides, we have $\ln \frac{I(t)}{I(0)} = \rho st$. Taking the antilog (letting each side become the exponent of e), we have

$$\exp\left[\ln \frac{I(t)}{I(0)}\right] = \exp(\rho st)$$

or $\quad \frac{I(t)}{I(0)} = e^{\rho st}$

or $\quad I(t) = I(0)e^{\rho st}$

CHAPTER 14

Exercise 14.1

1 (a) With $a = 4$ and $b = 12$, we have $y_c = Ae^{-4t}$, $y_p = \frac{12}{4} = 3$. The general solution is $y(t) = Ae^{-4t} + 3$. Setting $t = 0$, we get $y(0) = A + 3$, thus $A = Y(0) - 3 = 2 - 3 = -1$. The definite solution is $y(t) = -e^{-4t} + 3$.

(b) $y_c = Ae^{-(-2)t}$, $y_p = \frac{0}{-2} = 0$. The general solution is $y(t) = Ae^{2t}$. Setting $t = 0$, we have $y(0) = A$; i.e., $A = 9$. Thus the definite solution is $y(t) = 9e^{2t}$.

(c) $y_c = Ae^{-10t}$, $y_p = \frac{15}{10} = \frac{3}{2}$. Thus $y(t) = Ae^{-10t} + \frac{3}{2}$. Setting $t = 0$, we get $y(0) = A + \frac{3}{2}$; i.e., $A = y(0) - \frac{3}{2} = 0 - \frac{3}{2} = -\frac{3}{2}$. The definite solution is $y(t) = \frac{3}{2}(1 - e^{-10t})$.

(d) Upon dividing through by 2, we get the equation $\frac{dy}{dt} + 2y = 3$. Hence $y_c = Ae^{-2t}$, $y_p = \frac{3}{2}$, and $y(t) = Ae^{-2t} + \frac{3}{2}$. Setting $t = 0$, we get $y(0) = A + \frac{3}{2}$, implying that $A = y(0) - \frac{3}{2} = 0$. The definite solution is $y(t) = \frac{3}{2}$.

3 (a) $y(t) = (0 - 4)e^{-t} + 4 = 4(1 - e^{-t})$

(b) $y(t) = 1 + 23t$

(c) $y(t) = (6 - 0)e^{5t} + 0 = 6e^{5t}$

(d) $y(t) = (4 - \frac{2}{3})e^{-3t} + \frac{2}{3} = 3\frac{1}{3}e^{-3t} + \frac{2}{3}$

(e) $y(t) = [7 - (-1)]e^{7t} + (-1) = 8e^{7t} - 1$

(f) After dividing by 3 throughout, we find the solution to be

$$y(t) = (0 - \frac{5}{6})e^{-2t} + \frac{5}{6} = \frac{5}{6}(1 - e^{-2t})$$

Exercise 14.2

1 The D curve should be steeper than the S curve. This means that $|-\beta| > |\delta|$, or $-\beta < \delta$, which is precisely the criterion for dynamic stability.

2 From (14.9), we may write $\alpha + \gamma = (\beta + \delta)\overline{P}$. Hence (14.10') can be rewritten as $\frac{dP}{dt} + j(\beta + \delta)P = j(\beta + \delta)\overline{P}$, or $\frac{dP}{dt} + kP = k\overline{P}$, or $\frac{dP}{dt} + k(P - \overline{P}) = 0$. By (14.3'), the time path corresponding to this homogeneous differential equation is $\Delta(t) = \Delta(0)e^{-kt}$. If $\Delta(0) = 0$, then $\Delta(t) = 0$; i.e., $P(t) = \overline{P}$. If $\Delta(0) \neq 0$, then $\Delta(t) \equiv P(t) - \overline{P}$ will converge to zero if and only if $k > 0$. This conclusion is no different from the one stated in the text.

3 The price adjustment equation (14.10) is what introduces a derivative (pattern of change) into the model, thereby generating a differential equation.

4 (a) By substitution, we have $\frac{dP}{dt} = j(Q_d - Q_s) = j(\alpha + \gamma) - j(\beta + \delta)P + j\sigma\frac{dP}{dt}$. This can be simplified to

$$\frac{dP}{dt} + \frac{j(\beta + \delta)}{1 - j\sigma}P = \frac{j(\alpha + \gamma)}{1 - j\sigma} \qquad (1 - j\sigma \neq 0)$$

The general solution is, by (14.5),

$$P(t) = A \exp\left[-\frac{j(\beta + \delta)}{1 - j\sigma}t\right] + \frac{\alpha + \gamma}{\beta + \delta}$$

(b) Since $dP/dt = 0$ iff $Q_d = Q_s$, the intertemporal equilibrium price is the same as the market-clearing equilibrium price $(= \frac{\alpha + \gamma}{\beta + \delta})$.

(c) Condition for dynamic stability: $1 - j\sigma > 0$, or $\sigma < \frac{1}{j}$.

5 (a) Setting $Q_d = Q_s$, and simplifying, we have

$$\frac{dP}{dt} + \frac{\beta + \delta}{\eta}P = \frac{\alpha}{\eta}$$

The general solution is, by (14.5),

$$P(t) = A \exp\left(-\frac{\beta + \delta}{\eta}t\right) + \frac{\alpha}{\beta + \delta}$$

(b) Since $-(\beta + \delta)/\eta$ is negative, the exponential term tends to zero, as t tends to infinity. The intertemporal equilibrium is dynamically stable.

(c) Although there lacks a dynamic adjustment mechanism for price, the demand function contains a dP/dt term. This gives rise to a differential equation and makes the model dynamic.

Exercise 14.3

We shall omit all constants of integration in this Exercise.

1 Since $u = 5$, $w = 15$, and $\int u\,dt = 5t$, solution formula (14.15) gives

$$y(t) = e^{-5t}(A + \int 15e^{5t}\,dt) = e^{-5t}(A + 3e^{5t}) = Ae^{-5t} + 3$$

The same result can be obtained also by using formula (14.5).

2 Since $u = 2t$, $w = 0$ and $\int u\,dt = t^2$, solution formula (14.14) gives us $y(t) = Ae^{-t^2}$.

3 Since $u = 2t$, $w = t$, and $\int u\,dt = t^2$, formula (14.15) yields

$$y(t) = e^{-t^2}(A + \int te^{t^2}\,dt) = e^{-t^2}(A + \frac{1}{2}e^{t^2}) = Ae^{-t^2} + \frac{1}{2}$$

Setting $t = 0$, we find $y(0) = A + \frac{1}{2}$; i.e., $A = y(0) - \frac{1}{2} = 1$. Thus the definite solution is $y(t) = e^{-t^2} + \frac{1}{2}$.

4 Since $u = t^2$, $w = 5t^2$, and $\int u\,dt = t^3/3$, formula (14.15) gives us

$$y(t) = e^{-t^3/3}(A + \int 5t^2e^{t^3/3}\,dt) = e^{-t^3/3}(A + 5e^{t^3/3}) = Ae^{-t^3/3} + 5$$

Setting $t = 0$, we find $y(0) = A + 5$; thus $A = y(0) - 5 = 1$. The definite solution is $y(t) = e^{-t^3/3} + 5$.

5 Dividing through by 2, we get $\frac{dy}{dt} + 6y = -e^t$. Now with $u = 6$, $w = -e^t$, and $\int u\,dt = 6t$, formula (14.15) gives us

$$y(t) = e^{-6t}(A + \int -e^te^{6t}\,dt) = e^{-6t}(A - \frac{1}{7}e^{7t}) = Ae^{-6t} - \frac{1}{7}e^t$$

Setting $t = 0$, we find $y(0) = A - \frac{1}{7}$; i.e., $A = y(0) + \frac{1}{7} = 1$. The definite solution is $y(t) = e^{-6t} - \frac{1}{7}e^t$.

6 Since $u = 1$, $w = t$, and $\int u\,dt = t$, the general solution is

$$\begin{aligned} y(t) &= e^{-t}(A + \int te^t\,dt) \\ &= e^{-t}[A + e^t(t - 1)] \qquad \text{[by Example 17, Section 13.2]} \\ &= Ae^{-t} + t - 1 \end{aligned}$$

Exercise 14.4

1 (a) With $M = 2yt^3$ and $N = 3y^2t^2$, we have $\frac{\partial M}{\partial t} = 6yt^2 = \frac{\partial N}{\partial y}$.

Step i: $F(y,t) = \int 2yt^3\,dy + \psi(t) = y^2t^3 + \psi(t)$

Step ii: $\frac{\partial F}{\partial t} = 3y^2t^2 + \psi'(t) = N = 3y^2t^2$; thus $\psi'(t) = 0$

Step iii: $\psi(t) = \int 0\,dt = k$

Step iv: $F(y,t) = y^2t^3 + k$, so the general solution is

$$y^2t^3 = c \qquad \text{or} \qquad y(t) = \left(\frac{c}{t^3}\right)^{1/2}$$

(b) With $M = 3y^2t$ and $N = y^3 + 2t$, we have $\frac{\partial M}{\partial t} = 3y^2 = \frac{\partial N}{\partial y}$.

Step i: $F(y, t) = \int 3y^2t\,dy + \psi(t) = y^3t + \psi(t)$

Step ii: $\frac{\partial F}{\partial t} = y^3 + \psi'(t) = N = y^3 + 2t$; thus $\psi'(t) = 2t$

Step iii: $\psi(t) = \int 2t\,dt = t^2$ [constant omitted]

Step iv: $F(y,t) = y^3t + t^2$, so the general solution is

$$y^3t + t^2 = c \qquad \text{or} \qquad y(t) = \left(\frac{c - t^2}{t}\right)^{1/3}$$

(c) With $M = t(1 + 2y)$ and $N = y(1 + y)$, we have $\frac{\partial M}{\partial t} = 1 + 2y = \frac{\partial N}{\partial y}$.

Step i: $F(y,t) = \int t(1 + 2y)\,dy + \psi(t) = yt + y^2t + \psi(t)$

Step ii: $\frac{\partial F}{\partial t} = y + y^2 + \psi'(t) = N = y(1 + y)$; thus $\psi'(t) = 0$

Step iii: $\psi(t) = \int 0\,dt = k$

Step iv: $F(y,t) = yt + y^2t + k$, so the general solution is

$$yt + y^2t = c$$

(d) The equation can be rewritten as $4y^3t^2\,dy + (2y^4t + 3t^2)\,dt = 0$, with $M = 4y^3t^2$ and $N = 2y^4t + 3t^2$, so that $\frac{\partial M}{\partial t} = 8y^3t = \frac{\partial N}{\partial y}$.

Step i: $F(y,t) = \int 4y^3t^2\,dy + \psi(t) = y^4t^2 + \psi(t)$

Step ii: $\frac{\partial F}{\partial t} = 2y^4t + \psi'(t) = N = 2y^4t + 3t^2$; thus $\psi'(t) = 3t^2$

Step iii: $\psi(t) = \int 3t^2\,dt = t^3$ [constant omitted]

Step iv: $F(y,t) = y^4t^2 + t^3$, so the general solution is

$$y^4t^2 + t^3 = c \qquad \text{or} \qquad y(t) = \left(\frac{c - t^3}{t^2}\right)^{1/4}$$

2 (a) Inexact; y is an integrating factor.

(b) Inexact; t is an integrating factor.

3 Step i: $F(y, t) = \int M\,dy + \psi(t)$

Step ii: $\frac{\partial F}{\partial t} = \frac{\partial}{\partial t}\int M\,dy + \psi'(t) = N$; thus $\psi'(t) = N - \frac{\partial}{\partial t}\int M\,dy$

Step iii: $\psi(t) = \int\left(N - \frac{\partial}{\partial t}\int M\,dy\right)dt = \int N\,dt - \int\left(\frac{\partial}{\partial t}\int M\,dy\right)dt$

Step iv: $F(y, t) = \int M\,dy + \int N\,dt - \int\left(\frac{\partial}{\partial t}\int M\,dy\right)dt$

Setting $F(y, t) = c$, we obtain the desired result.

Exercise 14.5

1 (a) (1) Separable; we can write the equation as $\frac{2}{y}\,dy + \frac{2}{t}\,dt = 0$.

(2) Rewritten as $\frac{dy}{dt} + \frac{1}{t}\,y = 0$, the equation is linear.

(b) (1) Separable; multiplying by $(y + t)$, we get $y\,dy + 2t\,dt = 0$.

(2) Rewritten as $\frac{dy}{dt} = -2ty^{-1}$, the equation is a Bernoulli equation with $R = 0$, $T = -2t$ and $m = -1$. Define $z = y^{1-m} = y^2$. Then we can obtain from (14.24') a linearized equation

$$dz - 2(-2)t\,dt = 0 \qquad \text{or} \qquad \frac{dz}{dt} + 4t = 0$$

(c) (1) Separable; we can write the equation as $y\,dy + t\,dt = 0$.

(2) Reducible; it is a Bernoulli equation with $R = 0$, $T = -t$, and $m = -1$.

(d) (1) Separable; we can write the equation as $\frac{1}{3y^2}\,dy - t\,dt = 0$

(2) Yes; it is a Bernoulli equation with $R = 0$, $T = 3t$, $m = 2$.

2 (a) Integrating $\frac{2}{y}\,dy + \frac{2}{t}\,dt = 0$ after cancelling the common factor 2, we get $\ln y + \ln t = c$, or $\ln yt = c$. The solution is

$$yt = e^c = k \qquad \text{or} \qquad y(t) = k/t$$

Check: $\frac{dy}{dt} = -kt^{-2} = -\frac{y}{t}$ (consistent with the given equation).

(b) Cancelling the common factor $\frac{1}{y + t}$, and integrating, we get $\frac{1}{2}y^2 + t^2 = c$. Thus the solution is

$$y(t) = (2c - 2t^2)^{1/2} = (k - 2t^2)^{1/2}$$

Check: $\frac{dy}{dt} = \frac{1}{2}(k - 2t^2)^{-1/2}(-4t) = -\frac{2t}{y}$ (which is equivalent to the given differential equation).

3 Integrating $y\,dy + t\,dt = 0$, we get $\frac{1}{2}y^2 + \frac{1}{2}t^2 = c$, or $y^2 + t^2 = 2c = A$. Thus the solution is $y(t) = (A - t^2)^{1/2}$. Treating it as a Bernoulli equation with $R = 0$, $T = -t$, $m = -1$, and $z = y^{1-m} = y^2$, we can use formula (14.24') to obtain the linearized equation $dz + 2t\,dt = 0$, or $\frac{dz}{dt} = -2t$, which has the solution $z = A - t^2$. Reverse substitution then yields the identical answer

$$y^2 = A - t^2 \qquad \text{or} \qquad y(t) = (A - t^2)^{1/2}$$

4 Integrating $\frac{1}{3}y^{-2}\,dy - t\,dt = 0$, we obtain $-\frac{1}{3}y^{-1} - \frac{1}{2}t^2 = c$, or $y^{-1} = -3c - \frac{3}{2}t^2 = A - \frac{3}{2}t^2$. The solution is $y(t) = \frac{1}{A - \frac{3}{2}t^2}$.

Treating it as a Bernoulli equation, on the other hand, we have $R = 0$, $T = 3t$, and $m = 2$. Thus we can write $dz + 3t\,dt = 0$, or $\frac{dz}{dt} = -3t$, which has the solution $z = A - \frac{3}{2}t^2$. Since $z = y^{1-m} = y^{-1}$, we have $y(t) = \frac{1}{z}$, which represents an identical solution.

5 The derivative of the solution is $\frac{dz}{dt} = 2At + 2$. The linearized equation itself implies on the other hand that $\frac{dz}{dt} = \frac{2z}{t} - 2$. But since $z = At^2 + 2t$, the latter result amounts to $2(At + 2) - 2 = 2At + 2$. Thus the two results are identical.

<u>Exercise 14.6</u>

1 (a) and (d): The phase line is upward-sloping, and the equilibrium is accordingly dynamically unstable.

(b) and (c): The phase line is downward-sloping, and the equilibrium is dynamically stable.

2 (a) The phase line is upward-sloping for nonnegative y; the

equilibrium $\bar{y} = 3$ is dynamically unstable.

(b) The phase line slopes upward from the point of origin, reaches a peak at the point (1/4, 1/16), and then slopes downward thereafter. There are two equilibriums, $\bar{y} = 0$ and $\bar{y} = 1/2$; the former is dynamically unstable, but the latter is dynamically stable.

3 (a) An equilibrium can occur only when $dy/dt = 0$, i.e., only when $y = 3$, or $y = 5$.

(b) $$\frac{d}{dy}\left(\frac{dy}{dt}\right) = 2y - 8 = \begin{cases} -2 & \text{when } y = 3 \\ +2 & \text{when } y = 5 \end{cases}$$

Since this derivative measures the slope of the phase line, we can infer that the equilibrium at $y = 3$ is dynamically stable, but the equilibrium at $y = 5$ is dynamically unstable.

Exercise 14.7

1 Upon dividing by k throughout, the equation becomes

$$\frac{\dot{k}}{k} = \frac{s\phi(k)}{k} - \lambda$$

Since the first term on the right is equal to $\frac{sQ/L}{K/L} = \frac{sQ}{K} = \frac{\dot{K}}{K}$, the equation above means that:

growth rate of $\frac{K}{L}$ = growth rate of K - growth rate of L

2 $I \equiv \frac{dK}{dt} = \frac{d}{dt} Ae^{\lambda t} = A\lambda e^{\lambda t} = Be^{\lambda t}$. Thus net investment, I, obviously also grows at the rate λ.

3 The rate of growth of Q should be the sum of the rates of growth of T(t) and of f(K, L). The former rate is given to be ρ; the latter rate is λ. Hence we have $r_Q = \rho + \lambda$.

4 The assumption of linear homogeneity (constant returns to scale) is what enables us to focus on the capital-labor ratio.

5 (a)

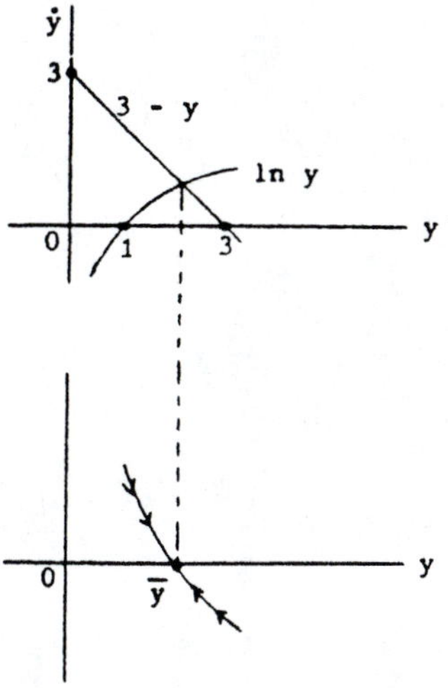

There is a single equilibrium $\bar{y}$ which lies between 1 and 3, and is dynamically stable.

(b)

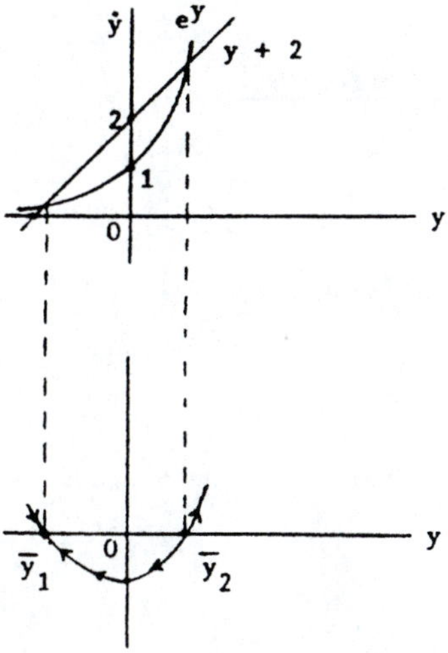

There are two equilibriums: $\bar{y}_1$ (negative) is dynamically stable, and $\bar{y}_2$ (positive) is dynamically unstable.

CHAPTER 15

Exercise 15.1

1 (a) By (15.3), $y_p = \frac{b}{a_2} = \frac{2}{5}$ (b) By (15.3'), $y_p = \frac{bt}{a_1} = 7t$

(c) By (15.3), $y_p = 9/3 = 3$ (d) By (15.3), $y_p = -4/-1 = 4$

(e) By (15.3"), $y_p = \frac{bt^2}{2} = 6t^2$

2 (a) With $a_1 = 3$ and $a_2 = -4$, we find $r_1, r_2 = \frac{1}{2}(-3 \pm 5) = 1, -4$.

Thus $y_c = A_1e^t + A_2e^{-4t}$.

(b) With $a_1 = 6$ and $a_2 = 5$, we find $r_1, r_2 = \frac{1}{2}(-6 \pm 4) = -1, -5$.

Thus $y_c = A_1e^{-t} + A_2e^{-5t}$.

(c) With $a_1 = -2$ and $a_2 = 1$, we get repeated roots $r_1 = r_2 = 1$.

Thus, by (15.9), $y_c = A_3e^t + A_4te^t$.

(d) With $a_1 = 8$ and $a_2 = 16$, we find $r_1 = r_2 = -4$. Thus we have

$y_c = A_3e^{-4t} + A_4te^{-4t}$.

3 (a) By (15.3), $y_p = -3$. Adding this to the earlier-obtained y_c, we get the general solution $y(t) = A_1e^t + A_2e^{-4t} - 3$. Setting $t = 0$ in this solution, and using the first initial condition, we have $y(0) = A_1 + A_2 - 3 = 4$. Differentiating $y(t)$ and then setting $t = 0$, we find via the second initial condition that $y'(0) = A_1 - 4A_2 = 2$. Thus $A_1 = 6$ and $A_2 = 1$. The definite solution is $y(t) = 6e^t + e^{-4t} - 3$.

(b) $y_p = 2$. The general solution is $y(t) = A_1e^{-t} + A_2e^{-5t} + 2$. The initial conditions give us $y(0) = A_1 + A_2 + 2 = 4$, and $y'(0) = -A_1 - 5A_2 = 2$. Thus $A_1 = 3$ and $A_2 = -1$. The definite solution is $y(t) = 3e^{-t} - e^{-5t} + 2$.

(c) $y_p = 3$. The general solution is $y(t) = A_3e^t + A_4te^t + 3$. Since $y(0) = A_3 + 3 = 4$, and $y'(0) = 1 + A_4 = 2$, we have $A_3 = 1$, and $A_4 = 1$. The definite solution is $y(t) = e^t + te^t + 3$.

(d) $y_p = 0$. The general solution is $y(t) = A_3e^{-4t} + A_4te^{-4t}$.

Since $y(0) = A_3 = 4$, and $y'(0) = -4A_3 + A_4 = 2$, we have $A_3 = 4$ and $A_4 = 18$. Thus the definite solution is $y(t) = 4e^{-4t} + 18te^{-4t}$.

4 (a) Unstable. (b) Stable. (c) Unstable. (d) Stable.

5 (a) Setting $t = 0$ in the solution, we get $y(0) = 2 + 0 + 3 = 5$. This satisfies the first initial condition. The derivative of the solution is $y'(t) = -6e^{-3t} - 3te^{-3t} + e^{-3t}$, implying that $y'(0) = -6 - 0 + 1 = -5$. This checks with the second initial condition.

(b) The second derivative is $y''(t) = 18e^{-3t} + 9te^{-3t} - 3e^{-3t} - 3e^{-3t} = 12e^{-3t} + 9te^{-3t}$. Substitution of the expressions for y'', y' and y into the left side of the differential equation yields the value 27, since all exponential terms cancel out. Thus the solution is validated.

6 For the case of $r < 0$, we first rewrite te^{rt} as t/e^{-rt}, where both the numerator and the denominator tend to infinity as t tends to infinity. Thus, by L'Hôpital's rule,

$$\lim_{t\to\infty} \frac{t}{e^{-rt}} = \lim_{t\to\infty} \frac{1}{-re^{-rt}} = 0 \qquad \text{(case of } r < 0\text{)}$$

For the case of $r > 0$, both the component t and the component e^{rt} will tend to infinity as t tends to infinity. Thus their product te^{rt} will also tend to infinity.

For the case of $r = 0$, we have $te^{rt} = te^0 = t$. Thus te^{rt} tends to infinity as t tends to infinity.

Exercise 15.2

1 (a) $r_1, r_2 = \frac{1}{2}(3 \pm \sqrt{-27}) = \frac{3}{2} \pm \frac{3}{2}\sqrt{3}\, i$

(b) $r_1, r_2 = \frac{1}{2}(-2 \pm \sqrt{-64}) = -1 \pm 8i$

(c) $x_1, x_2 = \frac{1}{4}(-1 \pm \sqrt{-63}) = -\frac{1}{4} \pm \frac{3}{4}\sqrt{7}i$

(d) $x_1, x_2 = \frac{1}{4}(1 \pm \sqrt{-7}) = \frac{1}{4} \pm \frac{1}{4}\sqrt{7}i$

2 (a) Since 180 degrees = 3.14159 radians,

$$1 \text{ radian} = \frac{180}{3.14159} \text{ degrees} = 57.3 \text{ degrees (or } 57°18'\text{)}$$

(b) Similarly, 1 degree $= \frac{3.14159}{180}$ radians = 0.01745 radians.

3 (a) $\sin^2\theta + \cos^2\theta \equiv (\frac{v}{R})^2 + (\frac{h}{R})^2 \equiv \frac{v^2 + h^2}{R^2} \equiv 1$, because R is defined to be $(v^2 + h^2)^{1/2}$. This result is true regardless of the value of θ; hence we use the identity sign.

(b) When $\theta = \frac{\pi}{4}$, we have v = h, so $R = \sqrt{2v^2} = v\sqrt{2}$ (= $h\sqrt{2}$).

Thus, $\sin\frac{\pi}{4} = \cos\frac{\pi}{4} = \frac{v}{R} = \frac{v}{v\sqrt{2}} = \frac{1}{\sqrt{2}} = \frac{\sqrt{2}}{2}$.

4 (a) $\sin 2\theta \equiv \sin(\theta + \theta) \equiv \sin\theta\cos\theta + \cos\theta\sin\theta$

$\equiv 2\sin\theta\cos\theta$ [Here, $\theta_1 = \theta_2 = \theta$]

(b) $\cos 2\theta \equiv \cos(\theta + \theta) \equiv \cos\theta\cos\theta - \sin\theta\sin\theta \equiv \cos^2\theta$

$- \sin^2\theta \equiv \cos^2\theta + \sin^2\theta - 2\sin^2\theta \equiv 1 - 2\sin^2\theta$

(c) $\sin(\theta_1 + \theta_2) + \sin(\theta_1 - \theta_2) \equiv (\sin\theta_1\cos\theta_2 + \cos\theta_1\sin\theta_2)$

$+ (\sin\theta_1\cos\theta_2 - \cos\theta_1\sin\theta_2) \equiv 2\sin\theta_1\cos\theta_2$

(d) $1 + \tan^2\theta \equiv 1 + \frac{\sin^2\theta}{\cos^2\theta} \equiv \frac{\cos^2\theta + \sin^2\theta}{\cos^2\theta} \equiv \frac{1}{\cos^2\theta}$

(e) $\sin(\frac{\pi}{2} - \theta) \equiv \sin\frac{\pi}{2}\cos\theta - \cos\frac{\pi}{2}\sin\theta \equiv \cos\theta - 0 \equiv \cos\theta$

(f) $\cos(\frac{\pi}{2} - \theta) \equiv \cos\frac{\pi}{2}\cos\theta + \sin\frac{\pi}{2}\sin\theta \equiv 0 + \sin\theta \equiv \sin\theta$

5 (a) $\frac{d}{d\theta}\sin f(\theta) = \frac{d\sin f(\theta)}{df(\theta)}\frac{df(\theta)}{d\theta} = \cos f(\theta)\cdot f'(\theta) = f'(\theta)\cos f(\theta)$

$\frac{d}{d\theta}\cos f(\theta) = \frac{d\cos f(\theta)}{df(\theta)}\frac{df(\theta)}{d\theta} = \sin f(\theta)\cdot[-f'(\theta)]$

$= -f'(\theta)\sin f(\theta)$

(b) $\frac{d}{d\theta}\cos\theta^3 = -3\theta^2\sin\theta^3$

$\frac{d}{d\theta}\sin(\theta^2 + 3\theta) = (2\theta + 3)\cos(\theta^2 + 3\theta)$

$$\frac{d}{d\theta}\cos e^{\theta} = -e^{\theta}\sin e^{\theta}$$

$$\frac{d}{d\theta}\sin\frac{1}{\theta} = -\frac{1}{\theta^2}\cos\frac{1}{\theta}$$

6 (a) $e^{-i\pi} = \cos\pi - i\sin\pi = -1 - 0 = -1$

(b) $e^{i\pi/3} = \cos\frac{\pi}{3} + i\sin\frac{\pi}{3} = \frac{1}{2} + i\frac{\sqrt{3}}{2} = \frac{1}{2}(1 + \sqrt{3}\,i)$

(c) $e^{i\pi/4} = \cos\frac{\pi}{4} + i\sin\frac{\pi}{4} = \frac{1}{\sqrt{2}} + i\frac{1}{\sqrt{2}} = \frac{1}{\sqrt{2}}(1 + i) = \frac{\sqrt{2}}{2}(1 + i)$

(d) $e^{-3i\pi/4} = \cos\frac{3\pi}{4} - i\sin\frac{3\pi}{4} = -\frac{1}{\sqrt{2}} - i\frac{1}{\sqrt{2}} = -\frac{1}{\sqrt{2}}(1 + i)$

$$= -\frac{\sqrt{2}}{2}(1 + i)$$

7 (a) With $R = 2$ and $\theta = \frac{\pi}{6}$, we find $h = 2\cos\frac{\pi}{6} = \sqrt{3}$ and $v = 2\sin\frac{\pi}{6} = 1$. The cartesian form is $\sqrt{3} + i$.

(b) With $R = 4$ and $\theta = \frac{\pi}{3}$, we find $h = 4\cos\frac{\pi}{3} = 2$, and $v = 4\sin\frac{\pi}{3} = 2\sqrt{3}$. The cartesian form is $2 + 2\sqrt{3}i$.

(c) Taking the complex number as $\sqrt{2}e^{+i\theta}$, we have $R = \sqrt{2}$ and $\theta = -\frac{\pi}{4}$. So $h = \sqrt{2}\cos\frac{-\pi}{4} = \sqrt{2}\cos\frac{\pi}{4}$ [by (15.14)] $= 1$, and $v = \sqrt{2}\sin\frac{-\pi}{4} = \sqrt{2}(-\sin\frac{\pi}{4}) = -1$. The cartesian form is $h + vi = 1 - i$.

Alternatively, taking the number as $\sqrt{2}e^{-i\theta}$, we would have $\theta = \frac{\pi}{4}$ instead, with the result that $h = v = 1$. The cartesian form is then $h - vi = 1 - i$, the same answer.

8 (a) With $h = \frac{3}{2}$ and $v = \frac{3\sqrt{3}}{2}$, we find $R = 3$. Since θ must satisfy $\cos\theta = \frac{h}{R} = \frac{1}{2}$ and $\sin\theta = \frac{v}{R} = \frac{\sqrt{3}}{2}$, Table 15.2 gives us $\theta = \frac{\pi}{3}$. Thus, $\frac{3}{2} + \frac{3\sqrt{3}}{2}i = 3(\cos\frac{\pi}{3} + i\sin\frac{\pi}{3}) = 3e^{i\pi/3}$.

(b) With $h = 4\sqrt{3}$ and $v = 4$, we find $R = 8$. In order that $\cos\theta = \frac{h}{R} = \frac{\sqrt{3}}{2}$ and $\sin\theta = \frac{v}{R} = \frac{1}{2}$, we must have $\theta = \frac{\pi}{6}$. Hence,

$$4(\sqrt{3} + i) = 8(\cos\frac{\pi}{6} + i\sin\frac{\pi}{6}) = 8e^{i\pi/6}.$$

Exercise 15.3

1 $a_1 = -4$, $a_2 = 8$, $b = 0$. Thus $y_p = 0$. Since $h = 2$, and $v = 2$, we have $y_c = e^{2t}(A_5 \cos 2t + A_6 \sin 2t)$. The general solution is the same as y_c, since $y_p = 0$. From this solution, we can find that $y(0) = A_5 \cos 0 + A_6 \sin 0 = A_5$, and $y'(0) = 2(A_5 + A_6)$. Since the initial conditions are $y(0) = 3$ and $y'(0) = 7$, we get $A_5 = 3$, and $A_6 = \frac{1}{2}$. The definite solution is therefore

$$y(t) = e^{2t}(3 \cos 2t + \frac{1}{2} \sin 2t)$$

2 $a_1 = 4, a_2 = 8$, $b = 2$. Thus $y_p = \frac{1}{4}$. Since $h = -2$ and $v = 2$, we have $y_c = e^{-2t}(A_5 \cos 2t + A_6 \sin 2t)$. The general solution is $y(t) = y_c + y_p$. From this solution, we can find $y(0) = A_5 + 1/4$, and $y'(0) = -2A_5 + 2A_6$, which, along with the initial conditions, imply that $A_5 = 2$ and $A_6 = 4$. Thus the definite solution is

$$y(t) = e^{-2t} (2\cos 2t + 4 \sin 2t) + \frac{1}{4}$$

3 $a_1 = 3$, $a_2 = 4$, $b = 12$. Thus $y_p = 3$. Since $h = -\frac{3}{2}$ and $v = \frac{\sqrt{7}}{2}$, we have $y_c = e^{-3t/2}(A_5 \cos \frac{\sqrt{7}}{2} t + A_6 \sin \frac{\sqrt{7}}{2} t)$. The general solution is $y(t) = y_c + y_p$. From this solution, we can find $y(0) = A_5 + 3$, and $y'(0) = -\frac{3}{2}A_5 + \frac{\sqrt{7}}{2}A_6$, which, along with the initial conditions, imply that $A_5 = -1$ and $A_6 = \frac{\sqrt{7}}{7}$. The definite solution is

$$y(t) = e^{-3t/2}(- \cos \frac{\sqrt{7}}{2}t + \frac{\sqrt{7}}{7} \sin \frac{\sqrt{7}}{2}t) + 3$$

4 $a_1 = -2$, $a_2 = 10$, $b = 5$. Thus $y_p = \frac{1}{2}$. Since $h = 1$ and $v = 3$, we have $y_c = e^t (A_5 \cos 3t + A_6 \sin 3t)$. The general solution is $y(t) = y_c + y_p$. From this solution, we can find $y(0) = A_5 + \frac{1}{2}$, and $y'(0) = A_5 + 3A_6$, which, in view of the initial conditions, imply that $A_5 = 5\frac{1}{2}$ and $A_6 = 1$. Thus the definite solution is

$$y(t) = e^t(5\tfrac{1}{2} \cos 3t + \sin 3t) + \frac{1}{2}$$

5 $a_1 = 0$, $a_2 = 9$, $b = 3$. Thus $y_p = \frac{1}{3}$. Also, $h = 0$, $v = 3$, and thus

$y_c = A_5 \cos 3t + A_6 \sin 3t$. The general solution is $y(t) = y_c + y_p$. From this solution, we can find $y(0) = A_5 + 1/3$, and $y'(0) = 3A_6$, which, by the initial conditions, imply that $A_5 = 2/3$ and $A_6 = 1$. Thus the definite solution is

$$y(t) = \frac{2}{3} \cos 3t + \sin 3t + \frac{1}{3}$$

6 After normalizing (dividing by 2), we have $a_1 = -6$, $a_2 = 10$, $b = 20$. Thus $y_p = 2$. Since $h = 3$ and $v = 1$, $y_c = e^{3t}(A_5 \cos t + A_6 \sin t)$. The general solution is $y(t) = y_c + y_p$. This solution yields $y(0) = A_5 + 2$ and $y'(0) = 3A_5 + A_6$, which, by the initial conditions, imply that $A_5 = 2$ and $A_6 = -1$. Thus the definite solution is

$$y(t) = e^{3t}(2 \cos t - \sin t) + 2$$

7 (a) 2 and 3 (b) 5 (c) 1, 4, and 6

Exercise 15.4

1 (a) Equating Q_d and Q_s, and normalizing, we have

$$P'' + \frac{m - u}{n - w} P' - \frac{\beta + \delta}{n - w} P = -\frac{\alpha + \gamma}{n - w} \qquad (n \neq w)$$

(b) $P_p = \dfrac{\alpha + \gamma}{\beta + \delta}$

(c) Periodic fluctuation will be absent if

$$\left(\frac{m - u}{n - w}\right)^2 \geq \frac{-4(\beta + \delta)}{n - w}$$

2 (a) Substitution of Q_d and Q_s into the market adjustment equation yields (upon normalization)

$$P'' + \frac{jm - 1}{jn} P' - \frac{\beta + \delta}{n} P = -\frac{\alpha + \gamma}{n}$$

(b) The equilibrium price (in both senses) $= \dfrac{\alpha + \gamma}{\beta + \delta}$.

(c) Fluctuation will occur if

$$\left(\frac{jm - 1}{jn}\right)^2 < \frac{-4(\beta + \delta)}{n}$$

This condition cannot be satisfied if $n > 0$, for then the

right-side expression will be negative, and the square of a real number can never be less than a negative number.

(d) For Case 3, dynamic stability requires that

$$h = -\frac{1}{2}\left(\frac{jm - 1}{jn}\right) < 0$$

Since $n < 0$ for Case 3, this condition reduces to

$$jm - 1 < 0$$

3 (a) Equating Q_d and Q_s, and normalizing, we get

$$P'' - P' + \frac{5}{2} P = 5$$

The particular integral is $P_p = 2$. The characteristic roots are complex, with $h = \frac{1}{2}$ and $v = \frac{3}{2}$. Thus the general solution is $P(t) = e^{t/2}(A_5 \cos \frac{3}{2} t + A_6 \sin \frac{3}{2} t) + 2$. This can be definitized to

$$P(t) = e^{t/2}(2 \cos \frac{3}{2} t + 2 \sin \frac{3}{2} t) + 2$$

(b) The path is nonconvergent, and has explosive fluctuation.

Exercise 15.5

1 (a) Substituting (15.33) into (15.34) yields a first-order differential equation in π:

$$\frac{d\pi}{dt} + j(1 - h)\pi = j(\alpha - T - \beta U)$$

(b) A first-order differential equation has only one characteristic root. Since fluctuation is produced by complex roots which come only in conjugate pairs, no fluctuation is now possible.

2 Differentiating (15.33) and (15.35), we get

$$\frac{dp}{dt} = -\beta \frac{dU}{dt} + h \frac{d\pi}{dt}$$

$$\frac{d^2U}{dt^2} = k \frac{dp}{dt}$$

Substitution yields

$$\frac{d^2U}{dt^2} = -k\beta \frac{dU}{dt} + kh \frac{d\pi}{dt} = -k\beta \frac{dU}{dt} + khj(p - \pi) \quad \text{[by (15.34)]}$$

To get rid of p and π, we note that (15.35) implies

$$p = \frac{1}{k}\frac{dU}{dt} + m$$

and (15.33) implies

$$\pi = \frac{p}{h} - \frac{1}{h}(\alpha - T - \beta U) = \frac{1}{h}\left(\frac{1}{k}\frac{dU}{dt} + m\right) - \frac{1}{h}(\alpha - T - \beta U)$$

Using these to eliminate p and π, and rearranging, we then get the desired differential equation in U:

$$\frac{d^2U}{dt^2} + [k\beta + j(1 - h)]\frac{dU}{dt} + (kj\beta)U = kj[\alpha - T - (1 - h)m]$$

3 (a) Under the new assumption, (15.33) can be solved for p, to yield

$$p = \frac{1}{1 - h}(\alpha - T - \beta U)$$

This gives the derivative

$$\frac{dp}{dt} = -\frac{\beta}{1 - h}\frac{dU}{dt} = \frac{\beta km}{1 - h} - \frac{\beta k}{1 - h}p \qquad \text{[by (15.35)]}$$

Thus we have the differential equation

$$\frac{dp}{dt} + \frac{\beta k}{1-h}p = \frac{\beta km}{1 - h}$$

(b) Substituting the p expression derived in (a) into (15.35), we obtain (upon rearranging)

$$\frac{dU}{dt} + \frac{k\beta}{1 - h}U = -km + \frac{k}{1 - h}(\alpha - T)$$

(c) These are first-order differential equations.

(d) It is necessary to have the restriction $h \neq 1$.

4 (a) The parameter values are $\beta = 3$, $h = \frac{1}{3}$, $j = \frac{3}{4}$ and $k = \frac{1}{2}$. So, with reference to (15.37"), we have

$$a_1 = 2 \qquad a_2 = \frac{9}{8} \qquad \text{and} \qquad b = \frac{9}{8}m$$

The particular integral is $b/a_2 = m$. The characteristic roots are complex, with $h = -1$ and $v = \frac{\sqrt{2}}{4}$. Thus the general solution for π is

$$\pi(t) = e^{-t}\left(A_5 \cos\frac{\sqrt{2}}{4}t + A_6 \sin\frac{\sqrt{2}}{4}t\right) + m$$

Substituting this solution and its derivative into (15.41), and solving for p, we get

$$p(t) = \frac{1}{3} e^{-t}[(\sqrt{2}\, A_6 - A_5) \cos \frac{\sqrt{2}}{4} t - (\sqrt{2}\, A_5 + A_6) \sin \frac{\sqrt{2}}{4} t] + m$$

The new version of (15.40) implies that $U(t) = \frac{1}{9}\pi - \frac{1}{3}p + \frac{1}{18}$.

Thus

$$U(t) = \frac{1}{9} e^{-t}[(2A_5 - \sqrt{2}\, A_6) \cos \frac{\sqrt{2}}{4} t + (\sqrt{2}\, A_5 + 2A_6) \sin \frac{\sqrt{2}}{4} t] + \frac{1}{18} - \frac{2}{9} m$$

(b) Yes; yes.

(c) $\overline{p} = m$; $\overline{U} = \frac{1}{18} - \frac{2}{9} m$

(d) Now $\overline{U}$ is functionally related to $\overline{p}$. The long-run Phillips curve is no longer vertical, but negatively sloped. The assumption $h = 1$ (the entire expected rate of inflation is built into the actual rate of inflation) is crucial for the vertical long-run Phillips curve.

Exercise 15.6

1 Given $y''(t) + ay'(t) + by = t^{-1}$, the variable term t^{-1} has successive derivatives involving t^{-2}, t^{-3}, ..., and giving an infinite number of forms. If we let

$$y(t) = B_1 t^{-1} + B_2 t^{-2} + B_3 t^{-3} + B_4 t^{-4} + \ldots$$

there is no end to the y(t) expression. Thus we cannot use it as the particular integral.

2 (a) Try y_p in the form of $y = B_1 t + B_2$. Then $y'(t) = B_1$ and $y''(t) = 0$. Substitution yields $B_1 t + (2B_1 + B_2) = t$, thus $B_1 = 1$; moreover, $2B_1 + B_2 = 0$, thus $B_2 = -2$. Hence, $y_p = t - 2$.

(b) Try y_p in the form of $y = B_1 t^2 + B_2 t + B_3$. Then we have $y'(t) = 2B_1 t + B_2$, and $y''(t) = 2B_1$. Substitution now yields $B_1 t^2 + (8B_1 + B_2)t + (2B_1 + 4B_2 + B_3) = 2t^2$; thus $B_1 = 2$,

$B_2 = -16$, and $B_3 = 60$. Hence, $y_p = 2t^2 - 16t + 60$.

(c) Try y_p in the form of $y = Be^t$. Then $y'(t) = y''(t) = Be^t$.

Substitution yields $4Be^t = e^t$; thus $B = \frac{1}{4}$. Hence, $y_p = \frac{1}{4} e^t$.

(d) Try y_p in the form of $y = B_1 \sin t + B_2 \cos t$. Then we have

$y'(t) = B_1 \cos t - B_2 \sin t$, and $y''(t) = - B_1 \sin t - B_2 \cos t$.

Substitution yields $(2B_1 - B_2) \sin t + (B_1 + 2B_2) \cos t = \sin t$;

Thus $B_1 = \frac{2}{5}$, and $B_2 = -\frac{1}{5}$. Hence, $y_p = \frac{2}{5} \sin t - \frac{1}{5} \cos t$.

Exercise 15.7

1 (a) Since $a_n \neq 0$, we have $y_p = b/a_n = 8/2 = 4$.

(b) Since $a_n = 0$, but $a_{n-1} \neq 0$, we get $y_p = bt/a_{n-1} = \frac{t}{3}$.

(c) $a_n = a_{n-1} = 0$, but $a_{n-2} \neq 0$. We try the solution $y = kt^2$, so that $y'(t) = 2kt$, $y''(t) = 2k$, and $y'''(t) = 0$. Substitution yields $18k = 1$, or $k = 1/18$. Hence, $y_p = \frac{1}{18} t^2$.

(d) We again try $y = kt^2$, so that $y''(t) = 2k$ and $y^{(4)}(t) = 0$. Substitution yields $2k = 4$, or $k = 2$. Hence, $y_p = 2t^2$.

2 (a) $y_p = 4/2 = 2$. The characteristic roots are real and distinct, with values 1, -1, and 2. Thus the general solution is

$$y(t) = A_1e^t + A_2e^{-t} + A_3e^{2t} + 2$$

(b) $y_p = 0$. The roots are -1, -3, and -3 (repeated). Thus

$$y(t) = A_1e^{-t} + A_2e^{-3t} + A_3te^{-3t}$$

(c) $y_p = 8/8 = 1$. The roots are -4, and $-1+ i$, and $-1 - i$. Thus

$$y(t) = A_1e^{-4t} + e^{-t}(A_2 \cos t + A_3 \sin t) + 1$$

3 (a) There are two positive roots; the time path is divergent. To use the Routh theorem, we have $a_0 = 1$, $a_1 = -2$, $a_2 = -1$, $a_3 = 2$, and $a_4 = a_5 = 0$. The first determinant is $|a_1| = a_1 = -2 < 0$. Thus the condition for convergence is violated.

(b) All roots are negative; the time path is convergent. Applying the Routh theorem, we have $a_0 = 1$, $a_1 = 7$, $a_2 = 15$, $a_3 = 9$, and $a_4 = a_5 = 0$. The first three determinants have the values 7, 96, and 864, respectively. Thus covergence is assured.

(c) All roots have negative real parts; the time path is convergent. To use the Routh theorem, we have $a_0 = 1$, $a_1 = 6$, $a_2 = 10$, and $a_3 = 8$. The first three determinants have the values 6, 52, and 416, respectively. Thus convergence is again assured.

4 (a) Applying the Routh theorem, we have $a_0 = 1$, $a_1 = -10$, $a_2 = 27$, and $a_3 = -18$. The first determinant is $|a_1| = -10 < 0$. Thus the time path must be divergent.

(b) $a_0 = 1$, $a_1 = 11$, $a_2 = 34$, and $a_3 = 24$. The first three determinants are all positive (having the values 11, 350, and 8400, respectively). Hence the path is convergent.

(c) $a_0 = 1$, $a_1 = 4$, $a_2 = 5$, and $a_3 = -2$. The first three determinants have the values 4, 22, and -44, respectively. Since the last determinant is negative, the path is not convergent.

5 The Routh theorem requires that

$$|a_1| = a_1 > 0$$

and $$\begin{vmatrix} a_1 & a_3 \\ a_0 & a_2 \end{vmatrix} = \begin{vmatrix} a_1 & 0 \\ 1 & a_2 \end{vmatrix} = a_1a_2 > 0$$

With $a_1 > 0$, this last requirement implies that $a_2 > 0$, too.

CHAPTER 16

Exercise 16.2

1 (a) $y_{t+1} = y_t + 7$ (b) $y_{t+1} = 1.3y_t$ (c) $y_{t+1} = 3y_t - 9$

2 (a) Iteration yields $y_1 = y_0 + 1$, $y_2 = y_1 + 1 = y_0 + 2$, $y_3 = y_2 + 1 = y_0 + 3$, etc. The solution is $y_t = y_0 + t = 10 + t$.

(b) Since $y_1 = \alpha y_0$, $y_2 = \alpha y_1 = \alpha^2 y_0$, $y_3 = \alpha y_2 = \alpha^3 y_0$, etc., the solution is $y_t = \alpha^t y_0 = \beta\alpha^t$.

(c) Iteration yields $y_1 = \alpha y_0 - \beta$, $y_2 = \alpha y_1 - \beta = \alpha^2 y_0 - \alpha\beta - \beta$, $y_3 = \alpha y_2 - \beta = \alpha^3 y_0 - \alpha^2\beta - \alpha\beta - \beta$, etc. The solution is

$$y_t = \alpha^t y_0 - \beta(\underbrace{\alpha^{t-1} + \alpha^{t-2} + \dots + \alpha + 1}_{\text{a total of } t \text{ terms}})$$

3 (a) $y_{t+1} - y_t = 1$, so that $a = -1$ and $c = 1$. By (16.9'), the solution is $y_t = y_0 + ct = 10 + t$. The answer checks.

(b) $y_{t+1} - \alpha y_t = 0$, so that $a = -\alpha$, and $c = 0$. Assuming $\alpha \neq 1$, (16.8') applies, and we have $y_t = y_0\alpha^t = \beta\alpha^t$. It checks. [Assuming $\alpha = 1$ instead, we find from (16.9') that $y_t = \beta$, which is a special case of $y_t = \beta\alpha^t$.]

(c) $y_{t+1} - \alpha y_t = -\beta$, so that $a = -\alpha$, and $c = -\beta$. Assuming $\alpha \neq 1$, we find from (16.8') that $y_t = (y_0 + \frac{\beta}{1-\alpha})\alpha^t - \frac{\beta}{1-\alpha}$. This is equivalent to the earlier answer, because we can rewrite it as

$$y_t = y_0\alpha^t - \beta\left(\frac{1-\alpha^t}{1-\alpha}\right) = y_0\alpha^t - \beta(1 + \alpha + \alpha^2 + \dots + \alpha^{t-1})$$

4 (a) To find y_c, try the solution $y_t = Ab^t$ in the homogeneous equation $y_{t+1} + 3y_t = 0$. The result is $Ab^{t+1} + 3Ab^t = 0$; i.e., $b = -3$. Hence $y_c = Ab^t = A(-3)^t$. To find y_p, try the solution $y_t = k$ in the complete equation, to get $k + 3k = 4$; i.e., $k = 1$. Hence $y_p = 1$. The general solution is $y_t = A(-3)^t + 1$. Setting $t = 0$ in this solution, we get $y_0 = A + 1$. The initial

condition then gives us A = 3. The definite solution is

$y_t = 3(-3)^t + 1$.

(b) After normalizing the equation to $y_{t+1} - \frac{1}{2} y_t = 3$, we can find $y_c = Ab^t = A(\frac{1}{2})^t$, and $y_p = k = 6$. Thus $y_t = A(\frac{1}{2})^t + 6$. Using the initial condition, we get A = 1. The definite solution is $y_t = (\frac{1}{2})^t + 6$.

(c) After rewriting the equation as $y_{t+1} - 0.2y_t = 4$, we can find $y_c = A(0.2)^t$, and $y_p = 5$. Thus $y_t = A(0.2)^t + 5$. Using the initial condition, this solution can be definitized to $y_t = -(0.2)^t + 5$.

Exercise 16.3

1 (a) Nonoscillatory; divergent.

(b) Nonoscillatory; convergent (to zero).

(c) Oscillatory; convergent.

(d) Nonoscillatory; convergent.

2 (a) From the expression $3(-3)^t$, we have b = -3 (region VII). Thus the path will oscillate explosively around $y_p = 1$.

(b) With b = 1/2 (region III), the path will show a nonoscillatory movement from 7 toward $y_p = 2$.

(c) With b = 0.2 (region III again), we have another convergent, nonoscillatory path. But this time it goes upward from an initial value of 1 toward $y_p = 10$.

3 (a) a = -1/3, c = 6, $y_0 = 1$. By (16.8'), we have $y_t = -8(\frac{1}{3})^t + 9$ --nonoscillatory and convergent.

(b) a = 2, c = 9, $y_0 = 4$. By (16.8'), we have $y_t = (-2)^t + 3$ --oscillatory and divergent.

(c) a = 1/4, c = 5, $y_0 = 2$. By (16.8'), we find $y_t = -2(\frac{-1}{4})^t + 4$

--oscillatory and convergent.

(d) $a = -1$, $c = 3$, $y_0 = 5$. By (16.9'), we find $y_t = 5 + 3t$ --nonoscillatory and divergent (from a moving equilibrium 3t).

Exercise 16.4

1 Substitution of time path (16.12') into the demand equation leads to the time path of Q_{dt}, which we can simply write as Q_t (since $Q_{dt} = Q_{st}$ by the equilibrium condition):

$$Q_t = \alpha - \beta P_t = \alpha - \beta(P_0 - \overline{P})(-\frac{\delta}{\beta})^t - \beta\overline{P}$$

Whether Q_t converges depends on the $(-\frac{\delta}{\beta})^t$ term, which determines the convergence of P_t as well. Thus P_t and Q_t must be either both convergent, or both divergent.

2 The cobweb in this case will follow a specific rectangular path.

3 (a) $\alpha = 18$, $\beta = 3$, $\gamma = 3$, $\delta = 4$. Thus $\overline{P} = 21/7 = 3$. Since $\delta > \beta$, there is explosive oscillation.

(b) $\alpha = 22$, $\beta = 3$, $\gamma = 2$, $\delta = 1$. Thus $\overline{P} = 24/4 = 6$. Since $\delta < \beta$, the oscillation is damped.

(c) $\alpha = 19$, $\beta = 6$, $\gamma = 5$, $\delta = 6$. Thus $\overline{P} = 24/12 = 2$. Since $\delta = \beta$, there is uniform oscillation.

4 (a) The interpretation is that if actual price P_{t-1} exceeds (falls short of) the expected price P^*_{t-1}, then P^*_{t-1} will be revised upward (downward) by a fraction of the discrepancy $P_{t-1} - P^*_{t-1}$, to form the expected price of the next period, P^*_t. The adjustment process is essentially the same as in (15.34), except that, here, time is discrete, and the variable is price rather than the rate of inflation.

(b) If $\eta = 1$, then $P^*_t = P_{t-1}$ and the model reduces to the cobweb model (16.10). Thus the present model includes the cobweb model as a special case.

(c) The supply function gives $P_t^* = (Q_{st} + \gamma)/\delta$, which implies that $P_{t-1}^* = (Q_{s,t-1} + \gamma)/\delta$. But since $Q_{st} = Q_{dt} = \alpha - \beta P_t$, and similarly, $Q_{s,t-1} = \alpha - \beta P_{t-1}$, we have

$$P_t^* = \frac{\alpha + \gamma - \beta P_t}{\delta} \qquad \text{and} \qquad P_{t-1}^* = \frac{\alpha + \gamma - \beta P_{t-1}}{\delta}$$

Substituting these into the adaptive expectations equation, and simplifying and shifting the time subscript by one period, we obtain the equation

$$P_{t+1} - (1 - \eta - \frac{\eta\delta}{\beta})P_t = \frac{\eta(\alpha + \gamma)}{\beta}$$

which is in the form of (16.6) with $a = -(1 - \eta - \frac{\eta\delta}{\beta}) \neq -1$, and $c = \frac{\eta(\alpha + \gamma)}{\beta}$.

(d) Since $a \neq -1$, we can apply formula (16.8'), to get

$$P_t = (P_0 - \frac{\alpha + \gamma}{\beta + \delta})(1 - \eta - \frac{\eta\delta}{\beta})^t + \frac{\alpha + \gamma}{\beta + \delta}$$

$$= (P_0 - \overline{P})(1 - \eta - \frac{\eta\delta}{\beta})^t + \overline{P}$$

This time path is not necessarily oscillatory, but it will be if $(1 - \eta - \frac{\eta\delta}{\beta})$ is negative, i.e., if $\frac{\beta}{\beta + \delta} < \eta$.

(e) If the price path is oscillatory and convergent (region V in Fig. 16.1), we must have $-1 < 1 - \eta - \frac{\eta\delta}{\beta} < 0$, where the second inequality has to do with the presence of oscillation, and the first, with the question of convergence. Adding $(\eta - 1)$, and dividing through by η, we have $1 - \frac{2}{\eta} < -\frac{\delta}{\beta} < 1 - \frac{1}{\eta}$. Given that the path is oscillatory, convergence requires $1 - \frac{2}{\eta} < -\frac{\delta}{\beta}$. If $\eta = 1$ (cobweb model), the stability-inducing range for $-\frac{\delta}{\beta}$ is $-1 < -\frac{\delta}{\beta} < 0$. If $0 < \eta < 1$, however, the range will become wider. With $\eta = \frac{1}{2}$, e.g., the range becomes $-3 < -\frac{\delta}{\beta} < -1$.

5 The dynamizing agent is the lag in the supply function. This introduces P_{t-1} into the model, which together with P_t, forms a pattern of change.

Exercise 16.5

1 Because $a = \sigma(\beta + \delta) - 1 \neq -1$, by model specification.

2 (IV) $1 - \sigma(\beta + \delta) = 0$. Thus $\sigma = \frac{1}{\beta + \delta}$.

(V) $-1 < 1 - \sigma(\beta + \delta) < 0$. Subtracting 1, we get $-2 < -\sigma(\beta + \delta) < -1$. Multiplying by $\frac{-1}{\beta + \delta}$, we obtain $\frac{2}{\beta + \delta} > \sigma > \frac{1}{\beta + \delta}$.

(VI) $1 - \sigma(\beta + \delta) = -1$. Thus $\sigma = \frac{2}{\beta + \delta}$.

(VII) $1 - \sigma(\beta + \delta) < -1$. Subtracting 1, and multiplying by $\frac{-1}{\beta + \delta}$, we obtain $\sigma > \frac{2}{\beta + \delta}$.

3 With $\sigma = 0.3$, $\alpha = 21$, $\beta = 2$, $\gamma = 3$ and $\delta = 6$, we find from (16.15) that $P_t = (P_0 - 3)(-1.4)^t + 3$, a case of explosive oscillation.

4 The difference equation will become $P_{t+1} - (1 - \sigma\beta)P_t = \sigma(\alpha - k)$, with solution

$$P_t = (P_0 - \frac{\alpha - k}{\beta})(1 - \sigma\beta)^t + \frac{\alpha - k}{\beta}$$

The term $b^t = (1 - \sigma\beta)^t$ is decisive in the time-path configuration:

Region	b	σ
III	$0 < b < 1$	$0 < \sigma < \frac{1}{\beta}$
IV	$b = 0$	$\sigma = \frac{1}{\beta}$
V	$-1 < b < 0$	$\frac{1}{\beta} < \sigma < \frac{2}{\beta}$
VI	$b = -1$	$\sigma = \frac{2}{\beta}$
VII	$b < -1$	$\sigma > \frac{2}{\beta}$

[These results are the same as Table 16.2 with δ set equal to 0.]

To have a positive $\overline{P}$, we must have $k < \alpha$; that is, the horizontal supply curve must be located below the vertical intercept of the demand curve.

Exercise 16.6

1 No, y_t and y_{t+1} can take any real values, and are continuous.

2 (a) Yes, L and R give two equilibria.

(b) Nonoscillatory, explosive downward movement.

(c) Damped, steady upward movement toward R.

(d) Damped, steady downward movement toward R.

(e) L is an unstable equilibrium; R is a stable one.

3 (a) Yes.

(b) Nonoscillatory explosive decrease.

(c) At first there will be steady movement to the right, but as it approaches R, oscillation will develop because of the negative slope of the phase line. Whether the oscillation will be explosive depends on the steepness of the negatively-sloped segment of the curve.

(d) Oscillation around R will again occur--either explosive, or damped, provided y_0 maps to a point on the phase line higher than L.

(e) L is definitely unstable. The stability of R depends on the steepness of the curve.

4 (a) The phase line will be downward-sloping at first, but will become horizontal at the level of P_m on the vertical axis.

(b) Yes; yes.

(c) Yes.

5 From equation (16.17), we can write for the kink point:

$$\hat{p} = \frac{\alpha + \gamma}{\beta} - \frac{\delta}{\beta} k \qquad \text{or} \qquad \frac{\delta}{\beta} k = \frac{\alpha + \gamma}{\beta} - \hat{p}$$

It follows that

$$k = \frac{\beta}{\delta} \left(\frac{\alpha + \gamma}{\beta} - \hat{p}\right) = \frac{\alpha + \gamma}{\delta} - \frac{\beta}{\delta} \hat{p}$$

CHAPTER 17

Exercise 17.1

1 (a) $b^2 - b + \frac{1}{2} = 0$; $b_1, b_2 = \frac{1}{2}(1 \pm \sqrt{1-2}) = \frac{1}{2} \pm \frac{1}{2}i$.

(b) $b^2 - 4b + 4 = 0$; $b_1, b_2 = \frac{1}{2}(4 \pm \sqrt{16-16}) = 2, 2$.

(c) $b^2 + \frac{1}{2}b - \frac{1}{2} = 0$; $b_1, b_2 = \frac{1}{2}(-\frac{1}{2} \pm \sqrt{\frac{1}{4} + \frac{8}{4}}) = \frac{1}{2}, -1$.

(d) $b^2 - 2b + 3 = 0$; $b_1, b_2 = \frac{1}{2}(2 \pm \sqrt{4-12}) = 1 \pm \sqrt{2}i$.

2 (a) Complex roots imply stepped fluctuation. Since the absolute value of the roots is $R = \sqrt{a_2} = \sqrt{1/2} < 1$, it is damped.

(b) With repeated roots greater than one, the path is nonoscillatory and explosive.

(c) The roots are real and distinct; -1 is the dominant root. Its negativity implies oscillation, and its unit absolute value implies that oscillation will eventually become uniform.

(d) The complex roots have an absolute value greater than 1: $R = \sqrt{3}$. Thus there is explosive stepped fluctuation.

3 (a) $a_1 = -1$, $a_2 = 1/2$, and $c = 2$. By (17.2), $y_p = \frac{2}{1/2} = 4$.

(b) $y_p = 7/1 = 7$ (c) $y_p = 5/1 = 5$ (d) $y_p = 4/2 = 2$

All of these represent stationary equilibria.

4 (a) $a_1 = 3$, $a_2 = -7/4$, and $c = 9$. $y_p = \frac{9}{1 + 3 - 7/4} = 4$. With characteristic roots $b_1, b_2 = \frac{1}{2}(-3 \pm \sqrt{9+7}) = \frac{1}{2}(-3 \pm 4) = \frac{1}{2}, -\frac{7}{2}$, the general solution is: $y_t = A_1(\frac{1}{2})^t + A_2(-\frac{7}{2})^t + 4$. Setting $t = 0$ in this solution, and using the initial condition $y_0 = 6$, we have $6 = A_1 + A_2 + 4$; thus $A_1 + A_2 = 2$. Next, setting $t = 1$, and using $y_1 = 3$, we have $3 = \frac{1}{2}A_1 - \frac{7}{2}A_2 + 4$; thus $\frac{1}{2}A_1 - \frac{7}{2}A_2 = -1$. These results give us $A_1 = \frac{3}{2}$, and $A_2 = \frac{1}{2}$. Therefore, the definite solution is

$$y_t = \frac{3}{2}(\frac{1}{2})^t + \frac{1}{2}(-\frac{7}{2})^t + 4$$

(b) $a_1 = -2$, $a_2 = 2$, and $c = 1$. $y_p = \frac{1}{1 - 2 + 2} = 1$. The roots are $b_1, b_2 = \frac{1}{2}(2 \pm \sqrt{4 - 8}) = 1 \pm i$, giving us $h = 1$ and $v = 1$. Since $R = \sqrt{2}$, we find from (17.9) and Table 15.2 that $\theta = \frac{\pi}{4}$. The general solution is: $y_t = (\sqrt{2})^t(A_5 \cos \frac{\pi}{4}t + A_6 \sin \frac{\pi}{4}t) + 1$. Setting $t = 0$, and using the condition $y_0 = 3$, we obtain $3 = (A_5 \cos 0 + A_6 \sin 0) + 1 = A_5 + 0 + 1$; thus $A_5 = 2$. Next, setting $t = 1$, and using $y_1 = 4$, we find $4 = \sqrt{2}(2 \cos \frac{\pi}{4} + A_6 \sin \frac{\pi}{4}) + 1 = \sqrt{2}(2/\sqrt{2} + A_6/\sqrt{2}) + 1 = 2 + A_6 + 1$; thus $A_6 = 1$. The definite solution is therefore

$$y_t = (\sqrt{2})^t(2 \cos \frac{\pi}{4} t + \sin \frac{\pi}{4} t) + 1$$

(c) $a_1 = -1$, $a_2 = \frac{1}{4}$, and $c = 2$. $y_p = \frac{2}{1 - 1 + 1/4} = 8$. With roots $b_1, b_2 = \frac{1}{2}(1 \pm \sqrt{1 - 1}) = \frac{1}{2}, \frac{1}{2}$ (repeated), the general solution is: $y_t = A_3(\frac{1}{2})^t + A_4 t(\frac{1}{2})^t + 8$. Using the initial conditions, we find $A_3 = -4$ and $A_4 = 2$. Thus the definite solution is

$$y_t = -4(\frac{1}{2})^t + 2t(\frac{1}{2})^t + 8$$

5 (a) The dominant root being -7/2, the time path will eventually be characterized by explosive oscillation.

(b) The complex roots imply stepped fluctuation. Since $R = \sqrt{2} > 1$, the fluctuation is explosive.

(c) The repeated roots lie between 0 and 1; the time path is thus nonoscillatory and convergent.

Exercise 17.2

1 (a) Subcase 1D

(b) Subcase 3D

(c) Subcase 1C

(d) Subcase 3C

2 (a) $b_1, b_2 = \frac{1}{2}\,[\gamma(1 + \alpha) \pm \sqrt{\gamma^2(1 + \alpha)^2 - 4\alpha\gamma}] = \frac{1}{2}(3.6 \pm \sqrt{1.76})$

$= 2.46,\ 1.13$ (approximately). The path should be divergent.

(c) $b_1, b_2 = \frac{1}{2}(1.08 \pm \sqrt{0.446}) = 0.87,\ 0.21$ (approximately). The path sould be convergent.

3 For Possibilities ii and iv, with either $b_1 = 1$, or $b_2 = 1$, we find $(1 - b_1)(1 - b_2) = 0$. Thus, by (17.16), $1 - \gamma = 0$, or $\gamma = 1$. For Possibility iii, with $b_1 > 1$ and b_2 a positive fraction, $(1 - b_1)(1 - b_2)$ is negative. Thus, by (17.16), $1 - \gamma < 0$, or $\gamma > 1$.

4 Case 3 is characterized by $\gamma < \frac{4\alpha}{(1 + \alpha)^2}$. If $\gamma \geq 1$, then it follows that $1 < \frac{4\alpha}{(1 + \alpha)^2}$. Multiplying through by $(1 + \alpha)^2$, and subtracting 4α from both sides, we get $1 - 2\alpha + \alpha^2 < 0$, which can be written as $(1 - \alpha)^2 < 0$. But this inequality is impossible, since the square of a real number can never be negative. Hence we cannot have $\gamma \geq 1$ in Case 3.

Exercise 17.3

1 (a) Shifting the time subscripts in (17.23) forward one period, we get

$$(1 + \beta k)p_{t+2} - [1 - j(1 - h)]p_{t+1} + j\beta U_{t+1} = \beta km + j(\alpha - T)$$

(b) Subtracting (17.23) from the above result, we have

$$(1 + \beta k)p_{t+2} - [2 + \beta k - j(1 - h)]p_{t+1} + [1 - j(1 - h)]p_t + j\beta(U_{t+1} - U_t) = 0$$

(c) Now we substitute (17.20) to obtain

$$(1 + \beta k)p_{t+2} - [1 + hj + (1 - j)(1 + \beta k)]p_{t+1} + [1 - j(1 - h)]p_t = j\beta km$$

(d) When we divide through by $(1 + \beta k)$, the result is (17.24).

2 Substituting (17.18) into (17.19) and collecting terms, we get

$$\pi_{t+1} - (1 - j + jh)\pi_t = j(\alpha - T) - j\beta U_t$$

Differencing this result yields

$$\pi_{t+2} - (2 - j + jh)\pi_{t+1} + (1 - j + jh)\pi_t = -j\beta(U_{t+1} - U_t)$$
$$= j\beta km - j\beta kp_{t+1} \quad \text{[by (17.20)]}$$

A forward-shifted version of (17.19) gives us

$$j\, p_{t+1} = \pi_{t+2} - (1 - j)\pi_{t+1}$$

Using this to eliminate the p_{t+1} term in the preceding result, we get

$$(1 + \beta k)\pi_{t+2} - [1 + jh + (1 - j)(1 - k\beta)]\pi_{t+1} + (1 - j + jh)\pi_t$$
$$= j\beta km$$

When normalized, this becomes a difference equation with the same constant coefficients and constant term as in (17.24).

3 Let $h > 1$. Then from (17.26) and (17.27), we still have $b_1 + b_2 > 0$ and $(1 - b_1)(1 - b_2) > 0$. But in (17.26') we note that b_1b_2 can now exceed one. This would make feasible Possibility v (Case 1), Possibility viii (Case 2), and Possibilities x and xi (Case 3), all of which imply divergence.

4 (a) The first line of (17.21) is still valid, but its second line now becomes

$$p_{t+1} - p_t = \beta k(m - p_t) + hj(p_t - \pi_t)$$

Consequently, (17.23) becomes

$$p_{t+1} - [1 - j(1 - h) - \beta k]p_t + j\beta U_t = \beta km + j(\alpha - T)$$

And (17.24) becomes

$$p_{t+2} - [2 - j(1 - h) - \beta k]p_{t+1} + [1 - j(1 - h)$$
$$- \beta k(1 - j)]p_t = j\beta km$$

(b) No, we still have $\overline{p} = m$.

(c) With $j = h = 1$, we have $a_1 = \beta k - 2$ and $a_2 = 1$. Thus

$$a_1^2 \gtreqless 4a_2 \quad \text{iff} \quad (\beta k - 2)^2 \gtreqless 4 \quad \text{iff} \quad \beta k \gtreqless 4$$

The value of βk marks off the three cases from one another.

(d) With $\beta k = 3$, the roots are complex, with $R = \sqrt{a_2} = 1$; the path has stepped fluctuation and is nonconvergent.

With $\beta k = 4$, we have repeated roots, with $b = -\frac{1}{2}(4 - 2) = -1$; the time path has nonconvergent oscillation.

With $\beta k = 5$, we have distinct real roots, $b_1, b_2 = \frac{1}{2}(-3 \pm \sqrt{5})$ $= -0.38, -2.62$; the time path has divergent oscillation.

Exercise 17.4

1 (a) $\Delta t = (t + 1) - t = 1$ (b) $\Delta^2 t = \Delta(\Delta t) = \Delta(1) = 0$

These results are similar to $\frac{d}{dt} t = 1$, and $\frac{d^2}{dt^2} = 0$.

(c) $\Delta t^3 = (t + 1)^3 - t^3 = 3t^2 + 3t + 1$.

This result is very much different from $\frac{d}{dt} t^3 = 3t^2$.

2 (a) $c = 1$, $m = 3$, $a_1 = 2$ and $a_2 = 1$; (17.36) gives $y_p = \frac{1}{16}(3)^t$.

(b) Formula (17.36) does not apply since $m^2 + a_1 m + a_2 = 0$. We try the solution $y_t = Bt(6)^t$, and obtain the equation $B(t + 2)(6)^{t+2}$ $- 5B(t + 1)(6)^{t+1} - 6Bt(6)^t = 2(6)^t$. This reduces to $42B = 2$. Thus $B = \frac{1}{21}$ and $y_p = \frac{1}{21} t(6)^t$.

(c) After normalization, we find $c = 1$, $m = 4$, $a_1 = 0$ and $a_2 = 3$. By (17.36), we have $y_p = \frac{1}{19}(4)^t$.

3 (a) The trial solution is $y_t = B_0 + B_1 t$, which implies that y_{t+1} $= B_0 + B_1(t + 1) = (B_0 + B_1) + B_1 t$, and $y_{t+2} = B_0 + B_1(t + 2)$ $= (B_0 + 2B_1) + B_1 t$. Substitution into the difference equation yields $4B_0 + 4B_1 t = t$, so $B_0 = 0$ and $B_1 = \frac{1}{4}$. Thus $y_p = \frac{1}{4} t$.

(b) This is the same equation as in (a) except for the variable term. With the same trial solution, we get by substitution $4B_0 + 4B_1 t = 4 + 2t$. Thus $B_0 = 1$ and $B_1 = \frac{1}{2}$, and $y_p = 1 + \frac{1}{2} t$.

(c) The trial solution is $y_t = B_0 + B_1 t + B_2 t^2$ (same as in Example

2). Substituting this (and the corresponding y_{t+1} and y_{t+2} forms) into the equation, we get

$$(8B_0 + 7B_1 + 9B_2) + (8B_1 + 14B_2)t + 8B_2t^2 = 18 + 6t + 8t^2$$

Thus $B_0 = 2$, $B_1 = -1$, $B_2 = 1$, and $y_p = 2 - t + t^2$.

4 Upon successive differencing, the m^t part of the variable term gives rise to expressions in the form $B(m)^t$, whereas the t^n part leads to those in the form $(B_0 + \ldots + B_nt^n)$. The trial solution must take both of these into account.

5 (a) The characteristic equation is $b^3 - \frac{1}{2}b^2 - b + \frac{1}{2} = 0$, which can be written as $(b - \frac{1}{2})(b^2 - 1) = (b - \frac{1}{2})(b + 1)(b - 1) = 0$. The roots are $\frac{1}{2}$, -1, 1, and we have $y_c = A_1(\frac{1}{2})^t + A_2(-1)^t + A_3$.

(b) The characteristic equation is $b^3 - 2b^2 + \frac{5}{4}b - \frac{1}{4} = 0$, or $(b - \frac{1}{2})(b^2 - \frac{3}{2}b + \frac{1}{2}) = 0$. The first factor gives the root $\frac{1}{2}$; the second gives the roots 1 and $\frac{1}{2}$. Since two roots are repeated, we must write $y_c = A_1(\frac{1}{2})^t + A_2t(\frac{1}{2})^t + A_3$.

6 (a) Since $n = 2$, $a_0 = 1$, $a_1 = 1/2$ and $a_2 = -1/2$, we have

$$\Delta_1 = \begin{vmatrix} 1 & -1/2 \\ -1/2 & 1 \end{vmatrix} = \frac{3}{4} > 0, \text{ but } \Delta_2 = \begin{vmatrix} 1 & 0 & -1/2 & 1/2 \\ 1/2 & 1 & 0 & -1/2 \\ -1/2 & 0 & 1 & 1/2 \\ 1/2 & -1/2 & 0 & 1 \end{vmatrix} = 0$$

Thus the time path is not convergent.

(b) Since $a_0 = 1$, $a_1 = 0$ and $a_2 = -1/9$, we have

$$\Delta_1 = \begin{vmatrix} 1 & -1/9 \\ -1/9 & 1 \end{vmatrix} = \frac{80}{81}; \quad \Delta_2 = \begin{vmatrix} 1 & 0 & -1/9 & 0 \\ 0 & 1 & 0 & -1/9 \\ -1/9 & 0 & 1 & 0 \\ 0 & -1/9 & 0 & 1 \end{vmatrix} = \frac{6400}{6561}$$

The time path is convergent.

7 Since n = 3, there are three determinants as follows:

$$\Delta_1 = \begin{vmatrix} 1 & a_3 \\ a_3 & 1 \end{vmatrix} \qquad \Delta_2 = \begin{vmatrix} 1 & 0 & a_3 & a_2 \\ a_1 & 1 & 0 & a_3 \\ a_3 & 0 & 1 & a_1 \\ a_2 & a_3 & 0 & 1 \end{vmatrix}$$

$$\text{and} \qquad \Delta_3 = \begin{vmatrix} 1 & 0 & 0 & a_3 & a_2 & a_1 \\ a_1 & 1 & 0 & 0 & a_3 & a_2 \\ a_2 & a_1 & 1 & 0 & 0 & a_3 \\ a_3 & 0 & 0 & 1 & a_1 & a_2 \\ a_2 & a_3 & 0 & 0 & 1 & a_1 \\ a_1 & a_2 & a_3 & 0 & 0 & 1 \end{vmatrix}$$

CHAPTER 18

Exercise 18.2

1 The equation $y_{t+2} + 6y_{t+1} + 9y_t = 4$ is a specific example of (18.1), with $a_1 = 6$, $a_2 = 9$, and $c = 4$. When these values are inserted into (18.1'), we get precisely the system (18.4). The solution in Example 4 of Sec. 17.1 is exactly the same as that for the variable y obtained from the system (18.4), but it does not give the time path for x, since the variable x is absent from the single-equation formulation.

2 The characteristic equation of (18.2) can be written immediately as $b^3 + b^2 - 3b + 2 = 0$. As to (18.2'), the characteristic equation should be $|bI + K| = 0$; since $K = \begin{bmatrix} 1 & -3 & 2 \\ -1 & 0 & 0 \\ 0 & -1 & 0 \end{bmatrix}$, we have

$$|bI + K| = \begin{vmatrix} b+1 & -3 & 2 \\ -1 & b & 0 \\ 0 & -1 & b \end{vmatrix} = b^3 + b^2 - 3b + 2 = 0$$

which is exactly the same.

3 (a) To find the particular integrals, use (18.5'):

$$\begin{bmatrix} \bar{x} \\ \bar{y} \end{bmatrix} = (I + K)^{-1}d = \begin{bmatrix} 2 & 2 \\ 2 & -1 \end{bmatrix}^{-1} \begin{bmatrix} 24 \\ 9 \end{bmatrix} = \frac{1}{6}\begin{bmatrix} 1 & 2 \\ 2 & -2 \end{bmatrix} \begin{bmatrix} 24 \\ 9 \end{bmatrix} = \begin{bmatrix} 7 \\ 5 \end{bmatrix}$$

To find the complementary functions, we first form the characteristic equation by using (18.9'):

$$|bI + K| = \begin{vmatrix} b + 1 & 2 \\ 2 & b - 2 \end{vmatrix} = b^2 - b - 6 = 0$$

The roots $b_1 = 3$ and $b_2 = -2$ yield the following sets of m and n values: $m_1 = -A_1$, $n_1 = 2A_1$; $m_2 = 2A_2$, $n_2 = A_2$. Thus we have

$$x_c = -A_1(3)^t + 2A_2(-2)^t \qquad y_c = 2A_1(3)^t + A_2(-2)^t$$

Adding the particular integrals to these complementary functions, and definitizing the constants A_i, we finally get the time paths

$$x_t = -(3)^t + 4(-2)^t + 7 \qquad y_t = 2(3)^t + 2(-2)^t + 5$$

(b) The particular integrals can be found by setting all x's equal to $\overline{x}$ and all y's equal to $\overline{y}$, and solving the resulting equations. The answers are $\overline{x} = 6$, and $\overline{y} = 3$. If the matrix method is used, we must modify (18.5') by replacing I with $J = \begin{bmatrix} 1 & 0 \\ 1 & 1 \end{bmatrix}$. Thus

$$\begin{bmatrix} \overline{x} \\ \overline{y} \end{bmatrix} = (J + K)^{-1}d = \begin{bmatrix} 0 & -\frac{1}{3} \\ 1 & \frac{5}{6} \end{bmatrix}^{-1} \begin{bmatrix} -1 \\ 8\frac{1}{2} \end{bmatrix} = \begin{bmatrix} \frac{5}{2} & 1 \\ -3 & 0 \end{bmatrix} \begin{bmatrix} -1 \\ 8\frac{1}{2} \end{bmatrix} = \begin{bmatrix} 6 \\ 3 \end{bmatrix}$$

The characteristic equation, $|bJ + K| = \begin{vmatrix} b-1 & -\frac{1}{3} \\ b & b-\frac{1}{6} \end{vmatrix} = b^2 - \frac{5}{6}b + \frac{1}{6}$ $= 0$, has roots $b_1 = \frac{1}{2}$ and $b_2 = \frac{1}{3}$. These imply: $m_1 = 2A_1$, $n_1 = -3A_1$; $m_2 = A_2$, $n_2 = -2A_2$. Thus the complementary functions are

$$x_c = 2A_1 \left(\frac{1}{2}\right)^t + A_2 \left(\frac{1}{3}\right)^t \qquad y_c = -3A_1\left(\frac{1}{2}\right)^t - 2A_2\left(\frac{1}{3}\right)^t$$

Combining these with the particular integrals, and definitizing the constants A_i, we finally obtain the time paths

$$x_t = -2\left(\frac{1}{2}\right)^t + \left(\frac{1}{3}\right)^t + 6 \qquad y_t = 3\left(\frac{1}{2}\right)^t - 2\left(\frac{1}{3}\right)^t + 3$$

4 (a) To find the particular integrals, we utilize (18.14):

$$\begin{bmatrix} \overline{x} \\ \overline{y} \end{bmatrix} = M^{-1}g = \begin{bmatrix} -1 & -12 \\ 1 & 6 \end{bmatrix}^{-1} \begin{bmatrix} -60 \\ 36 \end{bmatrix} = \frac{1}{6} \begin{bmatrix} 6 & 12 \\ -1 & -1 \end{bmatrix} \begin{bmatrix} -60 \\ 36 \end{bmatrix} = \begin{bmatrix} 12 \\ 4 \end{bmatrix}$$

The characteristic equation, $|rI + M| = \begin{vmatrix} r-1 & -12 \\ 1 & r+6 \end{vmatrix} = r^2 + 5r$ $+ 6 = 0$, has roots $r_1 = -2$ and $r_2 = -3$. These imply: $m_1 = -4A_1$, $n_1 = A_1$; $m_2 = -3A_2$, $n_2 = A_2$. Thus the complementary functions are

$$x_c = -4A_1e^{-2t} - 3A_2e^{-3t} \qquad y_c = A_1e^{-2t} + A_2e^{-3t}$$

Combining these with the particular integrals, and definitizing the constants A_i, we find the time paths to be

$$x(t) = 4e^{-2t} - 3e^{-3t} + 12 \qquad y(t) = -e^{-2t} + e^{-3t} + 4$$

(b) The particular integrals are, according to (18.14),

$$\begin{bmatrix} \bar{x} \\ \bar{y} \end{bmatrix} = M^{-1}g = \begin{bmatrix} -2 & 3 \\ -1 & 2 \end{bmatrix}^{-1} \begin{bmatrix} 10 \\ 9 \end{bmatrix} = \begin{bmatrix} -2 & 3 \\ -1 & 2 \end{bmatrix} \begin{bmatrix} 10 \\ 9 \end{bmatrix} = \begin{bmatrix} 7 \\ 8 \end{bmatrix}$$

The characteristic equation, $|rI + M| = \begin{vmatrix} r-2 & 3 \\ -1 & r+2 \end{vmatrix} = r^2 - 1 = 0$,

has roots $r_1 = 1$ and $r_2 = -1$. These imply: $m_1 = 3A_1$, $n_1 = A_1$; $m_2 = A_2$, $n_2 = A_2$. Thus the complementary functions are

$$x_c = 3A_1e^t + A_2e^{-t} \qquad y_c = A_1e^t + A_2e^{-t}$$

Combining these with the particular integrals, and definitizing the constants A_i, we find the time paths to be

$$x(t) = 6e^t - 5e^{-t} + 7 \qquad y(t) = 2e^t - 5e^{-t} + 8$$

5 The system (18.13) is in the format of $Ju + Mv = g$, and the desired matrix is $D = -J^{-1}M$. Since $J^{-1} = \begin{bmatrix} 1 & -2 \\ 0 & 1 \end{bmatrix}$ and $M = \begin{bmatrix} 2 & 5 \\ 1 & 4 \end{bmatrix}$, we have $D = \begin{bmatrix} 0 & 3 \\ -1 & -4 \end{bmatrix}$. The characteristic equation of this matrix is $|D - rI| = 0$, or $\begin{vmatrix} -r & 3 \\ -1 & -4-r \end{vmatrix} = r^2 + 4r + 3 = 0$, which checks with (18.16').

<u>Exercise 18.3</u>

1 Since $d_t = \begin{bmatrix} \lambda_1 \\ \lambda_2 \end{bmatrix} \delta^t$, we have: $\begin{bmatrix} \delta-a_{11} & -a_{12} \\ -a_{21} & \delta-a_{22} \end{bmatrix} \begin{bmatrix} \beta_1 \\ \beta_2 \end{bmatrix} = \begin{bmatrix} \lambda_1 \\ \lambda_2 \end{bmatrix}$. Thus

$$\beta_1 = \frac{1}{\Delta}[\lambda_1(\delta - a_{22}) + \lambda_2 a_{12}] \qquad \beta_2 = \frac{1}{\Delta}[\lambda_2(\delta - a_{11}) + \lambda_1 a_{21}]$$

Where $\Delta \equiv (\delta - a_{11})(\delta - a_{22}) - a_{12}a_{21}$. It is clear that the answers in Example 1 are the special case where $\lambda_1 = \lambda_2 = 1$.

2 (a) The key to the rewriting process is the fact that

$$\delta I = \delta \begin{bmatrix} 1 & 0 \\ 0 & 1 \end{bmatrix} = \begin{bmatrix} \delta & 0 \\ 0 & \delta \end{bmatrix}.$$ The rest follows easily.

(b) Scalar: δ Vectors: β, u Matrices: I, A

(c) $\beta = (\delta I - A)^{-1}u$

3 (a) $\rho I + I - A = \begin{bmatrix} \rho & 0 \\ 0 & \rho \end{bmatrix} + \begin{bmatrix} 1 & 0 \\ 0 & 1 \end{bmatrix} - \begin{bmatrix} a_{11} & a_{12} \\ a_{21} & a_{22} \end{bmatrix}$

$= \begin{bmatrix} \rho + 1 - a_{11} & -a_{12} \\ -a_{21} & \rho + 1 - a_{22} \end{bmatrix}$. The rest follows easily.

(b) Scalar: ρ Vectors: β, λ Matrices: I, A.

(c) $\beta = (\rho I + I - A)^{-1}\lambda$

4 (a) With trial solution $\beta_i\delta^t = \beta_i(\frac{12}{10})^t$, we find from (18.22') that $\beta_1 = 70/39$ and $\beta_2 = 20/13$. So

$$x_{1p} = \frac{70}{39}(\frac{12}{10})^t \quad \text{and} \quad x_{2p} = \frac{20}{13}(\frac{12}{10})^t$$

(b) From the equation $\begin{vmatrix} b - \frac{3}{10} & -\frac{4}{10} \\ -\frac{3}{10} & b - \frac{2}{10} \end{vmatrix} = b^2 - \frac{5}{10}b - \frac{6}{100} = 0,$

We find $b_1, b_2 = \frac{6}{10}, -\frac{1}{10}$. These give us $m_1 = 4A_1$, $n_1 = 3A_1$, $m_2 = A_2$, $n_2 = -A_2$. Thus

$$x_{1c} = 4A_1(\frac{6}{10})^t + A_2(\frac{-1}{10})^t \quad \text{and} \quad x_{2c} = 3A_1(\frac{6}{10})^t - A_2(\frac{-1}{10})^t$$

(c) Combining the above results, and utilizing the initial conditions, we find $A_1 = 1$ and $A_2 = -1$. Thus the time paths are

$$x_{1,t} = 4(\frac{6}{10})^t - (-\frac{1}{10})^t + \frac{70}{39}(\frac{12}{10})^t$$

$$x_{2,t} = 3(\frac{6}{10})^t + (-\frac{1}{10})^t + \frac{20}{13}(\frac{12}{10})^t$$

5 (a) With the trial solution $\beta_i e^{\rho t} = \beta_i e^{t/10}$, we find from (18.25') that $\beta_1 = 17/6$ and $\beta_2 = 19/6$. Thus

$$x_{1p} = \frac{17}{6}e^{t/10} \quad \text{and} \quad x_{2p} = \frac{19}{6}e^{t/10}$$

(b) From the equation $\begin{vmatrix} r + 1 - \frac{3}{10} & -\frac{4}{10} \\ -\frac{3}{10} & r + 1 - \frac{2}{10} \end{vmatrix} = r^2 + \frac{15}{10}r + \frac{44}{100}$

$= 0$, we find $r_1 = -\frac{4}{10}$ and $r_2 = -\frac{11}{10}$. These give us $m_1 = 4A_1$,

$n_1 = 3A_1$, $m_2 = A_2$, and $n_2 = -A_2$. Thus

$$x_{1c} = 4A_1 e^{-4t/10} + A_2 e^{-11t/10}$$

$$x_{2c} = 3A_1 e^{-4t/10} - A_2 e^{-11t/10}$$

(c) Combining the above answers, and using the initial conditions, we get $A_1 = 1$ and $A_2 = 2$. The time paths are

$$x_1(t) = 4e^{-4t/10} + 2e^{-11t/10} + \frac{17}{6} e^{t/10}$$

$$x_2(t) = 3e^{-4t/10} - 2e^{-11t/10} + \frac{19}{6} e^{t/10}$$

6 (a) E, a and P are $n \times 1$ column vectors; A is an $n \times n$ matrix.

(b) The interpretation is that, at any instant of time, an excess demand for the ith product will induce a price adjustment to the extent of α_i times the magnitude of the excess demand.

(c) $dP_1/dt = \alpha_1(a_{10} + a_{11}P_1 + a_{12}P_2 + \dots + a_{1n}P_n)$

....

$dP_n/dt = \alpha_n(a_{n0} + a_{n1}P_1 + a_{n2}P_2 + \dots + a_{nn}P_n)$

(d) It can be verified that $P' = \alpha E$. Thus we have

$$P' = \alpha(a + AP) = \alpha a + \alpha AP$$

or
$$\underset{(n\times 1)}{P'} - \underset{(n\times n)}{\alpha}\ \underset{(n\times n)}{A}\ \underset{(n\times 1)}{P} = \underset{(n\times n)}{\alpha}\ \underset{(n\times 1)}{a}$$

7 (a) $E_{1,t} = a_{10} + a_{11}P_{1,t} + a_{12}P_{2,t} + \dots + a_{1n}P_{n,t}$

$E_{2,t} = a_{20} + a_{21}P_{1,t} + a_{22}P_{2,t} + \dots + a_{2n}P_{n,t}$

....

$E_{n,t} = a_{n0} + a_{n1}P_{1,t} + a_{n2}P_{2,t} + \dots + a_{nn}P_{n,t}$

Thus we have $E_t = a + AP_t$.

(b) Since $\Delta P_{i,t} \equiv P_{i,t+1} - P_{i,t}$, we can write

$$\begin{bmatrix} \Delta P_{1,t} \\ \vdots \\ \Delta P_{n,t} \end{bmatrix} = \begin{bmatrix} P_{1,t+1} - P_{1,t} \\ \vdots \\ P_{n,t+1} - P_{n,t} \end{bmatrix} = \underset{(n\times 1)}{P_{t+1}} - \underset{(n\times 1)}{P_t}$$

The rest follows easily.

(c) Inasmuch as $P_{t+1} - P_t = \alpha E_t = \alpha(a + AP_t) = \alpha a + \alpha AP_t$, it follows that

$$P_{t+1} - IP_t - \alpha AP_t = \alpha a$$

or $$P_{t+1} - (I + \alpha A)P_t = \alpha a$$

Exercise 18.4

1 Cramer's rule makes use of the determinants:

$$|A| = k\beta j \qquad |A_1| = j\beta km \qquad |A_2| = jk[\alpha - T - (1 - h)m]$$

Then we have: $\overline{\pi} = \dfrac{|A_1|}{|A|} = m, \qquad \overline{U} = \dfrac{|A_2|}{|A|} = \dfrac{\alpha - T - (1 - h)m}{\beta}$

2 The first equation in (18.34) gives us

$$-\frac{3}{4}(1 - i)m_1 = -\frac{9}{4}n_1$$

Multiplying through by $-\frac{4}{9}$, we get

$$\frac{1}{3}(1 - i)\,m_1 = n_1$$

The second equation in (18.34) gives us

$$-\frac{1}{2}m_1 = -\frac{3}{4}(1 + i)\,n_1$$

Multiplying through by $-\frac{2}{3}(1 - i)$, and noting that $(1 + i)(1 - i) = 1 - i^2 = 2$, we again get

$$\frac{1}{3}(1 - i)\,m_1 = n_1$$

3 (a) With $\alpha - T = 1/4$, $\beta = 2$, $h = 1$, $j = 1/2$ and $k = 1$, the system (18.28') becomes

$$\begin{bmatrix} 1 & 0 \\ 0 & 1 \end{bmatrix}\begin{bmatrix} \pi' \\ U' \end{bmatrix} + \begin{bmatrix} 0 & 1 \\ -1 & 2 \end{bmatrix}\begin{bmatrix} \pi \\ U \end{bmatrix} = \begin{bmatrix} \frac{1}{8} \\ \frac{1}{4} - m \end{bmatrix}$$

Setting $\pi' = U' = 0$, and solving, we get the particular integrals

$$\overline{\pi} = m \qquad \text{and} \qquad \overline{U} = \frac{1}{8}$$

Since the reduced equation (18.30) now becomes

$$\begin{bmatrix} r & 1 \\ -1 & r + 2 \end{bmatrix}\begin{bmatrix} m \\ n \end{bmatrix} = \begin{bmatrix} 0 \\ 0 \end{bmatrix}$$

The characteristic equation is $r^2 + 2r + 1 = 0$, with repeated real roots

$$r = r_1 = r_2 = -1$$

Using this value in the above matrix equation, we find the proportionality relation

$$m = n$$

Thus the complementary functions are

$$\begin{bmatrix} \pi_c \\ U_c \end{bmatrix} = \begin{bmatrix} A_3 e^{-t} + A_4 te^{-t} \\ A_3 e^{-t} + A_4 te^{-t} \end{bmatrix}$$

which, when added to the particular integrals, give the general solutions.

(b) With $\alpha - t = \frac{1}{6}$, $\beta = 2$, $h = \frac{1}{3}$, $j = \frac{1}{4}$ and $k = \frac{1}{2}$, the system (18.28') becomes

$$\begin{bmatrix} 1 & 0 \\ 0 & 1 \end{bmatrix} \begin{bmatrix} \pi' \\ U' \end{bmatrix} + \begin{bmatrix} \frac{1}{6} & \frac{1}{2} \\ -\frac{1}{6} & 1 \end{bmatrix} \begin{bmatrix} \pi \\ U \end{bmatrix} = \begin{bmatrix} \frac{1}{24} \\ \frac{1}{12} - \frac{m}{2} \end{bmatrix}$$

The particular integrals are

$$\overline{\pi} = m \qquad \text{and} \qquad \overline{U} = \frac{1}{12} - \frac{m}{3}$$

Since the reduced equation now becomes

$$\begin{bmatrix} r + \frac{1}{6} & \frac{1}{2} \\ -\frac{1}{6} & r + 1 \end{bmatrix} \begin{bmatrix} m \\ n \end{bmatrix} = \begin{bmatrix} 0 \\ 0 \end{bmatrix}$$

the characteristic equation is $r^2 + \frac{7}{6} r + \frac{1}{4} = 0$, with distinct real roots

$$r_1, r_2 = \frac{-7 \pm \sqrt{13}}{12}$$

Using r_1 and r_2 successively in the above matrix equation, we find

$$\frac{5 - \sqrt{13}}{6} m_1 = n_1 \qquad \text{and} \qquad \frac{5 + \sqrt{13}}{6} m_2 = n_2$$

Thus the complementary functions are

$$\begin{bmatrix}\pi_c\\U_c\end{bmatrix} = \begin{bmatrix}A_1\\ \frac{5-\sqrt{13}}{6}A_1\end{bmatrix}\exp\left(\frac{-7+\sqrt{13}}{12}t\right) + \begin{bmatrix}A_2\\ \frac{5+\sqrt{13}}{6}A_2\end{bmatrix}\exp\left(\frac{-7-\sqrt{13}}{12}t\right)$$

which, when added to the particular integrals, give the general solutions.

4 (a) With $\alpha - T = \frac{1}{2}$, $\beta = 3$, $h = \frac{1}{2}$, $j = \frac{1}{4}$ and $k = 1$, the system (18.36) becomes

$$\begin{bmatrix}1 & 0\\ -\frac{1}{2} & 4\end{bmatrix}\begin{bmatrix}\pi_{t+1}\\U_{t+1}\end{bmatrix} + \begin{bmatrix}-\frac{7}{8} & \frac{3}{4}\\ 0 & -1\end{bmatrix}\begin{bmatrix}\pi_t\\U_t\end{bmatrix} = \begin{bmatrix}\frac{1}{8}\\ \frac{1}{2}-m\end{bmatrix}$$

Letting $\overline{\pi} = \pi_t = \pi_{t+1}$ and $\overline{U} = U_t = U_{t+1}$, and solving, we get the particular integrals

$$\overline{\pi} = m \qquad \text{and} \qquad \overline{U} = \frac{1}{6}(1 - m)$$

Since the reduced equation (18.38) now becomes

$$\begin{bmatrix}b - \frac{7}{8} & \frac{3}{4}\\ -\frac{1}{2}b & 4b - 1\end{bmatrix}\begin{bmatrix}m\\n\end{bmatrix} = \begin{bmatrix}0\\0\end{bmatrix}$$

The charasteristic equation is $4b^2 - \frac{33}{8}b + \frac{7}{8} = 0$, with distinct real roots

$$b_1, b_2 = \frac{1}{64}(33 \pm \sqrt{193})$$

Using b_1 and b_2 successively in the matrix equation above, we find the proportionality relations

$$\frac{1}{48}(23 - \sqrt{193})\, m_1 = n_1 \qquad \text{and} \qquad \frac{1}{48}(23 + \sqrt{193})\, m_2 = n_2$$

Thus the complementary functions are

$$\begin{bmatrix}\pi_c\\U_c\end{bmatrix} = \begin{bmatrix}A_1\\ \frac{23-\sqrt{193}}{48}A_1\end{bmatrix}\left(\frac{33+\sqrt{193}}{64}\right)^t + \begin{bmatrix}A_2\\ \frac{23+\sqrt{193}}{48}A_2\end{bmatrix}\left(\frac{33-\sqrt{193}}{64}\right)^t$$

which, when added to the particular integrals, give the general solutions.

(b) With $\alpha - T = \frac{1}{4}$, $\beta = 4$, $h = 1$, $j = \frac{1}{4}$ and $k = 1$, the system (18.36) becomes

$$\begin{bmatrix} 1 & 0 \\ -1 & 5 \end{bmatrix} \begin{bmatrix} \pi_{t+1} \\ U_{t+1} \end{bmatrix} + \begin{bmatrix} -1 & 1 \\ 0 & -1 \end{bmatrix} \begin{bmatrix} \pi_t \\ U_t \end{bmatrix} = \begin{bmatrix} \frac{1}{16} \\ \frac{1}{4} - m \end{bmatrix}$$

The particular integrals are

$$\bar{\pi} = m \qquad \text{and} \qquad \bar{U} = \frac{1}{16}$$

Since the reduced equation (18.38) now becomes

$$\begin{bmatrix} b - 1 & 1 \\ -b & 5b - 1 \end{bmatrix} \begin{bmatrix} m \\ n \end{bmatrix} = \begin{bmatrix} 0 \\ 0 \end{bmatrix}$$

the characteristic equation is $5b^2 - 5b + 1 = 0$, with distinct real roots

$$b_1, b_2 = \frac{1}{2} \pm \frac{\sqrt{5}}{10}$$

Using these in the matrix equation above, we get

$$\left(\frac{1}{2} - \frac{\sqrt{5}}{10}\right) m_1 = n_1 \qquad \text{and} \qquad \left(\frac{1}{2} + \frac{\sqrt{5}}{10}\right) m_2 = n_2$$

Thus the complementary functions are

$$\begin{bmatrix} \pi_c \\ U_c \end{bmatrix} = \begin{bmatrix} A_1 \\ \left(\frac{1}{2} - \frac{\sqrt{5}}{10}\right) A_1 \end{bmatrix} \left(\frac{1}{2} + \frac{\sqrt{5}}{10}\right)^t + \begin{bmatrix} A_2 \\ \left(\frac{1}{2} + \frac{\sqrt{5}}{10}\right) A_2 \end{bmatrix} \left(\frac{1}{2} - \frac{\sqrt{5}}{10}\right)^t$$

which, when added to the particular integrals, give the general solutions.

Exercise 18.5

1 By introducing a new variable $x \equiv y'$ (which implies that $x' \equiv y''$), the given equation can be rewritten as the system

$$x' = f(x,y)$$

$$y' = x$$

which constitutes a special case of (18.40).

2 Since $\frac{\partial x'}{\partial y} = f_y > 0$, as y increases (moving northward in the phase space), x' will increase (x' will pass through three stages in its sign, in the order: $-$, 0, $+$). This yields the same conclusion as

$\frac{\partial x'}{\partial x}$. Similarly, $\frac{\partial y'}{\partial x} = g_x > 0$ yields the same conlusion as $\frac{\partial y'}{\partial y}$.

4 (a)

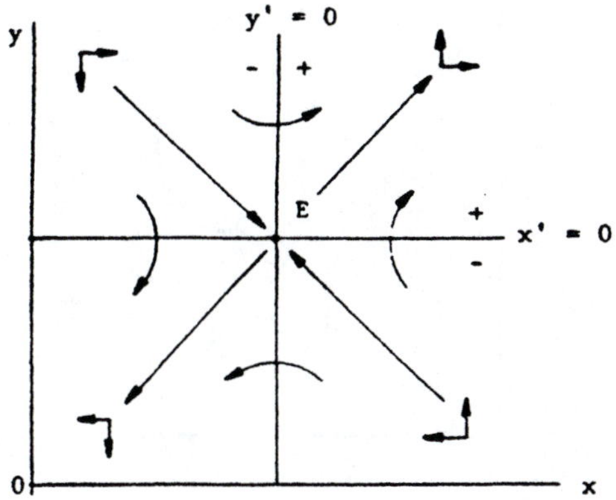

The x' = 0 curve has zero slope, and the y' = 0 curve has infinite slope. The equilibrium is a saddle point.

(b)

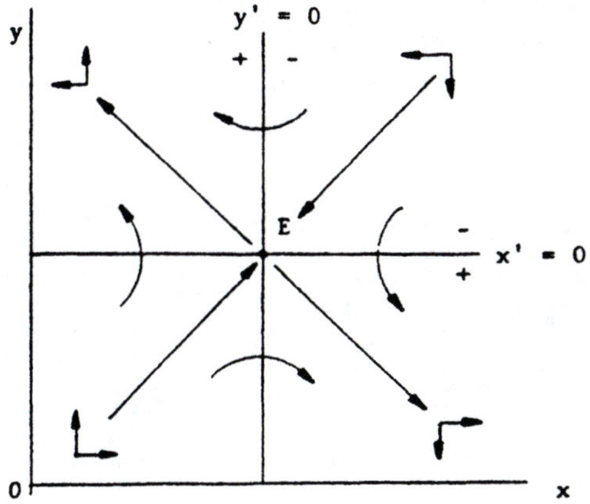

The equilibrium is also a saddle point.

5 (a) The partial-derivative signs imply that the x' = 0 curve is positively sloped, and the y' = 0 curve is negatively sloped.

Stable node:

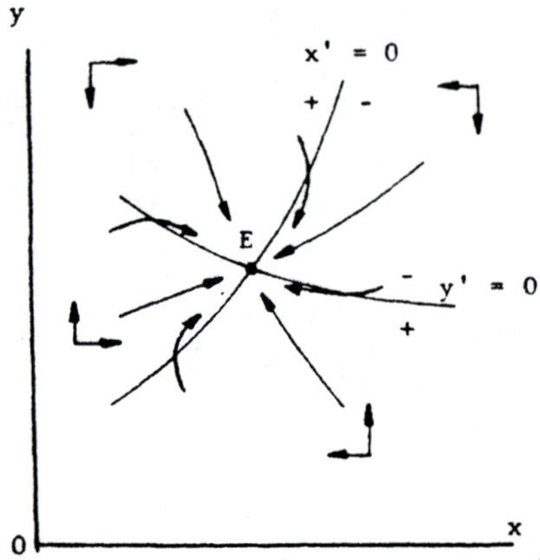

Stable focus:

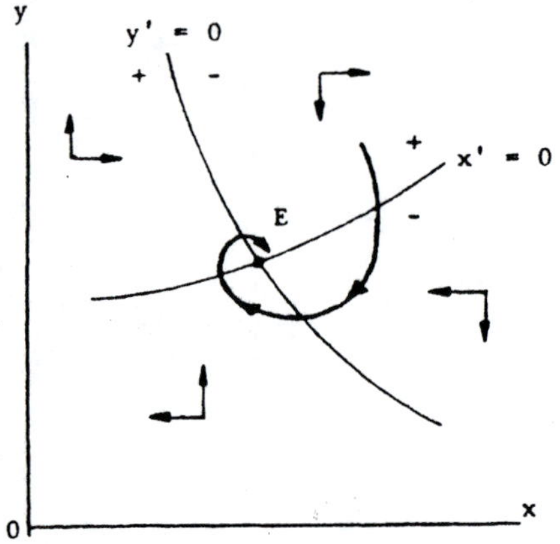

(b) A stable node results when a steep $x' = 0$ curve is coupled with a flat $y' = 0$ curve. A stable focus results if a flat $x' = 0$ curve is coupled with a steep $y' = 0$ curve.

<u>Exercise 18.6</u>

1 (a) The system has a unique equilibrium $E = (0, 0)$. The Jacobian evaluated at E is

$$J_e = \begin{bmatrix} e^x & 0 \\ ye^x & e^x \end{bmatrix}_{(0,\ 0)} = \begin{bmatrix} 1 & 0 \\ 0 & 1 \end{bmatrix}$$

Since $|J_E| = 1$ and $\text{tr}\, J_E = 2$, E is locally an unstable node.

(b) There are two equilibriums: $E_1 = (0, 0)$, and $E_2 = (\frac{1}{2}, -\frac{1}{4})$. The Jacobian evaluated at E_1 and E_2 yields

$$J_{E1} = \begin{bmatrix} 1 & 2 \\ 0 & 1 \end{bmatrix} \quad \text{and} \quad J_{E2} = \begin{bmatrix} 1 & 2 \\ 1 & 1 \end{bmatrix}$$

Since $|J_{E1}| = 1$ and $\text{tr}\, J_{E1} = 2$, E_1 is locally an unstable node. The second matrix has a negative determinant; thus E_2 is locally a saddle point.

(c) A single equilibrium exists at (0, 0). And

$$J_E = \begin{bmatrix} 0 & -e^y \\ 5 & -1 \end{bmatrix}_{(0,\ 0)} = \begin{bmatrix} 0 & -1 \\ 5 & -1 \end{bmatrix}$$

Since $|J_E| = 5$ and tr $J_E = -1$, the equilibrium is locally a stable focus.

(d) A single equilibrium exists at (0, 0). And

$$J_E = \begin{bmatrix} 3x^2 + 6xy & 3x^2 + 1 \\ 1 + y^2 & 2xy \end{bmatrix}_{(0,\ 0)} = \begin{bmatrix} 0 & 1 \\ 1 & 0 \end{bmatrix}$$

Since $|J_E| = -1$, the equilibrium is locally a saddle point.

2 (a) The elements of the Jacobian are signed as follows:

$\begin{bmatrix} 0 & + \\ + & 0 \end{bmatrix}$. Thus its determinant is negative, implying that the equilibrium is locally a saddle point.

(b) The Jacobian is in the form $\begin{bmatrix} 0 & - \\ - & 0 \end{bmatrix}$, and has a negative determinant. The equilibrium is, again, locally a saddle point.

(c) The Jacobian is in the form $\begin{bmatrix} - & + \\ - & - \end{bmatrix}$. Thus its determinant is positive, and its trace negative. The equilibrium is locally either a stable node or a stable focus.

3 The differential equations are

$$p' = h(1 - \mu)$$

$$\mu' = [p + q - m(p)]\mu \qquad m'(p) < 0$$

The equilibrium E occurs where $\overline{p} = p_1$ [where $p_1 = m(p_1) - q$ is the value of p that satisfies (18.56)] and $\overline{\mu} = 1$. The Jacobian is

$$J_E = \begin{bmatrix} 0 & -h \\ [1 - m'(p)]\mu & p + q - m(p) \end{bmatrix}_E = \begin{bmatrix} 0 & -h \\ 1 - m'(p_1) & 0 \end{bmatrix}$$

Since $|J_E| = h[1 - m'(p_1)] > 0$, and tr $J_E = 0$, the equilibrium is locally a vortex -- the same conclusion as in the phase-diagram analysis.

4 (a)

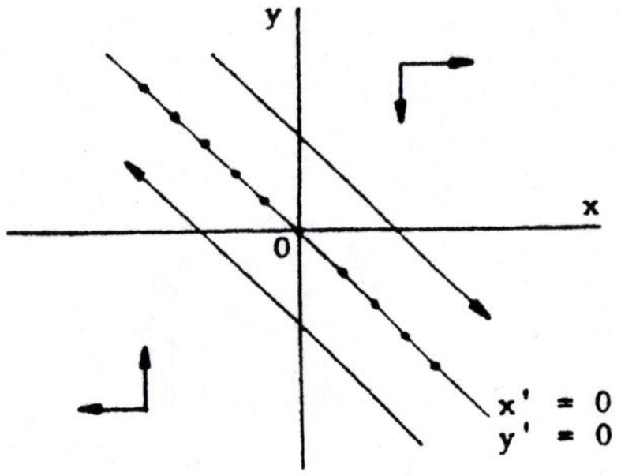

The x' = 0 and y' = 0 curves share the same equation y = -x. Thus the two curves coincide, to give rise to a lineful of equilibrium points. Initial points off that line do not lead to equilibrium.

(b)

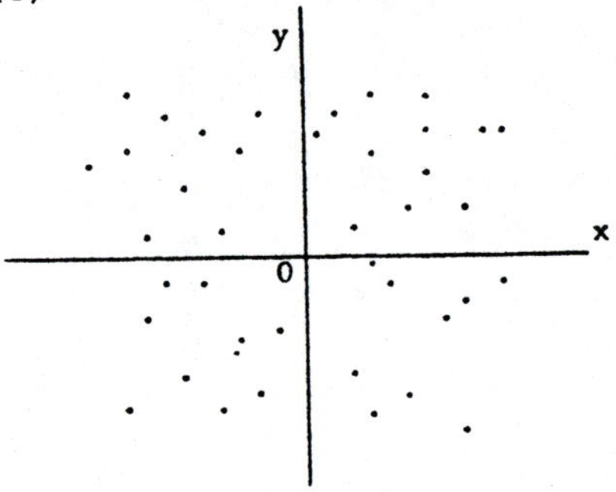

Since x' = y' = 0, neither x nor y can move. Thus any initial position can be considered as an equilibrium.

CHAPTER 19

Exercise 19.1

1 (a) $\bar{x}_1 = 2$, $\bar{x}_2 = 3$; $\bar{\pi} = 19$. (b) $\bar{x}_1 = 2$, $\bar{x}_2 = \frac{1}{2}$; $\bar{C} = 45$.

2 (a) Multiple optima: $2 \leq \bar{x}_1 \leq 4$ and $0 \leq \bar{x}_2 \leq \frac{1}{2}$, subject to $\bar{x}_1 + 4\bar{x}_2 = 4$. (Note: Each value of $\bar{x}_1$ is uniquely tied to a value of $\bar{x}_2$). An illustrative optimal solution is $\bar{x}_1 = 2$, $\bar{x}_2 = \frac{1}{2}$, with $\bar{C} = 24$. The multiple-optima situation arises because the objective function has the same slope as the second border.

(b) The optimal solution is unique: $\bar{x}_1 = 4$, $\bar{x}_2 = 0$, giving $\bar{C} = 24$. But only one variable (x_1) takes a nonzero optimal value. This is because the objective function is less steep than both of the borders.

3 Minimize $C = 6x_1 + 4x_2$

subject to

$$400x_1 + 100x_2 \geq 200$$
$$20x_1 + 10x_2 \geq 14$$
$$20x_1 + 60x_2 \geq 30$$
$$x_1 + x_2 = 1$$

and

$$x_1, x_2 \geq 0$$

Optimal solution: $\bar{x}_1 = 0.4$, $\bar{x}_2 = 0.6$, with $\bar{C} = \$4.80$ per gallon.

4 The objective function will become less steep in this case. We shall find that $\bar{x}_1 = 0.75$, and $\bar{x}_2 = 0.25$, with $\bar{C} = \$4.50$.

5 (a) The objective function will plot as a family of horizontal lines.

(b) The objective function will plot as a family of vertical lines.

(c) These two constraints together imply an equality constraint $ax_1 + bx_2 = c$. (Multiplying the second constraint by -1 yields $ax_1 + bx_2 \geq c$; combining this result with the first constraint yields the above equality.)

6 Maximize $\pi = x_1 + 6x_2$

subject to

$$800x_1 + 4000x_2 \leq 16{,}000$$
$$-x_1 \leq -5$$
$$x_2 \leq 4$$

and $x_1, x_2 \geq 0$

[The second constraint was originally $x_1 \geq 5$; we have multiplied it by -1, to unify the sense of inequality in the constraints.]

Optimal solution: $(\bar{x}_1, \bar{x}_2) = (5, 3)$.

7 No effect is produced, because the constraint is not binding and is automatically satisfied.

Exercise 19.2

1 Yes.

2 Yes, $\pi = c \cdot x$.

3 This equality can be replaced by two simultaneous inequalities:

$$a_{11}x_1 + a_{12}x_2 + \dots + a_{1n}x_n \geq r_1$$
$$a_{11}x_1 + a_{12}x_2 + \dots + a_{1n}x_n \leq r_1$$

Multiplying the second one by -1 will give us two "$\geq$" inequalities:

$$a_{11}x_1 + a_{12}x_2 + \dots + a_{1n}x_n \geq r_1$$
$$-a_{11}x_1 - a_{12}x_2 - \dots - a_{1n}x_n \geq -r_1$$

Exercise 19.4

1 (a) Maximize $\pi = 3x_1 + 2x_2 + 5x_3 + 0s_1 + 0s_2 + 0s_3$

subject to

$$3x_1 + x_2 + s_1 = 10$$
$$x_2 + 2x_3 + s_2 = 6$$
$$2x_1 + x_2 + x_3 + s_3 = 8$$

and $x_1, x_2, x_3, s_1, s_2, s_3 \geq 0$

(b) Minimize $C = x_1 + 6x_2 + 2x_3 + 0s_1 + 0s_2$

subject to

$$x_1 + 2x_2 - s_1 = 2$$
$$x_1 + x_2 + 3x_3 - s_2 = 12$$

and $x_1, x_2, x_3, s_1, s_2 \geq 0$

2 (a) Maximize $\pi = 2x_1 + 5x_2 + 0s_1 + 0s_2 + 0s_3$

subject to

$$x_1 + s_1 = 4$$
$$x_2 + s_2 = 3$$
$$x_1 + 2x_2 + s_3 = 8$$

and $x_1, x_2, s_1, s_2, s_3 \geq 0$

(b) Minimize $C = 12x_1 + 42x_2 + 0s_1 + 0s_2 + 0s_3$

subject to

$$x_1 + 2x_2 - s_1 = 3$$
$$x_1 + 4x_2 - s_2 = 4$$
$$3x_1 + x_2 - s_3 = 3$$

and $x_1, x_2, s_1, s_2, s_3 \geq 0$

3 (a) (0,0,4,3,8), (0,3,4,0,2), (2,3,2,0,0), (4,2,0,1,0),(4,0,0,3,4)

(b) (4,0,1,0,9), $(2,\frac{1}{2},0,0,\frac{7}{2})$, $(\frac{3}{5},\frac{6}{5},0,\frac{7}{5},0)$, (0,3,3,8,0)

4 There are 3 nonzero elements in each quintuple. No, this is the result of the presence of three constraints in each linear program involved (and nondegeneracy).

5 (b), (c), (d) and (e).

6 (a) The requirement space will be 3-dimensional, and the solution space 10-dimensional.

(b) 5-dimensional and 8-dimensional, respectively.

(c) m-dimensional and (m+n)-dimensional, respectively.

Exercise 19.5

1 The successive pivot elements are 2, and $\frac{1}{2}$ (row 1). The optimal solution is $(\bar{x}_1, \bar{x}_2, \bar{s}_1, \bar{s}_2) = (2, 2, 0, 0)$, with $\bar{\pi} = 14$.

2 The successive pivot elements are 3, and $\frac{1}{3}$. The optimal solution is $(\bar{x}_1, \bar{x}_2, \bar{s}_1, \bar{s}_2) = (2, 3, 0, 0)$, with $\bar{\pi} = 17$.

3 The successive pivot elements are 2 (x_1 column, row 1), and $\frac{3}{2}$ (x_3 column, row 2). The optimal solution is found to be $(\bar{x}_1, \bar{x}_2, \bar{x}_3, \bar{s}_1, \bar{s}_2, \bar{s}_3) = (4, 0, 2, 0, 0, 5)$, with $\bar{\pi} = 34$.

4 The successive pivot elements are 5, $\frac{3}{5}$, and 5. The optimal solution is $(\bar{x}_1, \bar{x}_2, \bar{x}_3, \bar{s}_1, \bar{s}_2, \bar{s}_3) = (2, 1, 3, 0, 0, 0)$, with $\bar{\pi} = 26$.

Exercise 19.6

2 First transform the simplex tableau into the form of Tableau II in Table 19.7. The successive pivot elements are then 3, $\frac{4}{3}$, and $\frac{1}{4}$. The optimal solution is $(\bar{x}_1, \bar{x}_2, \bar{s}_1, \bar{s}_2) = (8, 0, 0, 12)$, with $\bar{C} = 8$.

3 Only v_2 is needed here. Before pivoting, transform the simplex tableau by adding <u>twice row 1</u> plus <u>100 times row 2</u> to row 0. Then it takes only a single pivot step to reach the optimum, the pivot element being 1 (x_2 column, row 2). The optimal solution is $(\bar{x}_1, \bar{x}_2, \bar{s}_1, \bar{s}_2) = (2, 3, 0, 0)$, with $\bar{C} = 25$.

4 The seccessive pivot elements are 4, $\frac{11}{4}$, $\frac{5}{11}$, and $\frac{2}{5}$. The optimal solution is $(\bar{x}_1, \bar{x}_2, \bar{s}_1, \bar{s}_2, \bar{s}_3) = (2, \frac{1}{2}, 0, 0, \frac{7}{2})$, with $\bar{C} = 45$.

CHAPTER 20

Exercise 20.1

1 Minimize $\pi^* = 8y_1 + 14y_2$

subject to
$$\begin{bmatrix} 2 & 4 \\ 1 & 3 \end{bmatrix} \begin{bmatrix} y_1 \\ y_2 \end{bmatrix} \geq \begin{bmatrix} 9 \\ 1 \end{bmatrix}$$

and $y_1, y_2 \geq 0$

2 Maximize $C^* = 5y_1 + 4y_2 + 9y_3$

subject to
$$\begin{bmatrix} 1 & 0 & 2 \\ 2 & 1 & 3 \end{bmatrix} \begin{bmatrix} y_1 \\ y_2 \\ y_3 \end{bmatrix} \leq \begin{bmatrix} 1 \\ 7 \end{bmatrix}$$

and $y_i \geq 0 \quad (i = 1, 2, 3)$

3 Minimize $\pi^* = r_1y_1 + r_2y_2 + r_3y_3$

subject to
$$\begin{bmatrix} a_{11} & a_{21} & a_{31} \\ a_{12} & a_{22} & a_{32} \\ a_{13} & a_{23} & a_{33} \end{bmatrix} \begin{bmatrix} y_1 \\ y_2 \\ y_3 \end{bmatrix} \geq \begin{bmatrix} c_1 \\ c_2 \\ c_3 \end{bmatrix}$$

and $y_i \geq 0 \quad (i = 1, 2, 3)$

4 (a) Dual solution: $(\bar{y}_1, \bar{y}_2, \bar{t}_1, \bar{t}_2, \bar{t}_3) = (2, 3, 2, 0, 0)$

Primal solution: $(\bar{x}_1, \bar{x}_2, \bar{x}_3, \bar{s}_1, \bar{s}_2) = (0, 1, 2, 0, 0)$

(b) $\bar{C}^* = 2(2) + 5(3) = 19$; $\bar{C} = 4(0) + 3(1) + 8(2) = 19$. $\bar{C}^* = \bar{C}$.

5 (a) Yes, because no negative entries appear in row 0.

(b) $\bar{x}_1 = 2$, $\bar{x}_2 = 2$, with $\bar{\pi} = 14$.

(c) Two; because the primal has two dummy variables (there are two primal constraints).

(d) $\bar{y}_1 = 2$, $\bar{y}_2 = 1$, with $\bar{\pi}^* = 14$.

6 (a) $\bar{s}_1 = 0$, $\bar{s}_2 = 12$, and $\bar{C} = 8$.

(b) Maximize $C^* = 8y_1 + 12y_2$

subject to
$$\begin{bmatrix} 1 & 3 \\ 2 & 2 \end{bmatrix} \begin{bmatrix} y_1 \\ y_2 \end{bmatrix} \leq \begin{bmatrix} 1 \\ 4 \end{bmatrix}$$

and $y_1, y_2 \geq 0$

(c) $\overline{y}_2 = 0$; the first dual constraint is a strict equality.

(d) Since $y_1 + 3y_2 = 1$, and $\overline{y}_2 = 0$, we have $\overline{y}_1 = 1$.

(e) $\overline{C^*} = 8 = \overline{C}$.

7 (a) First replace the equality constraint with two inequalities

$$a_{21}x_1 + a_{22}x_2 \leq r_2$$

$$-a_{21}x_1 - a_{22}x_2 \leq -r_2$$

Then we can write the dual as:

Maximize $\quad C^* = r_1 y_1 + r_2 y_2 - r_2 y_3$

subject to $\quad a_{11}y_1 + a_{21}y_2 - a_{21}y_3 \leq c_1$

$\quad a_{12}y_1 + a_{22}y_2 - a_{22}y_3 \leq c_2$

and $\quad y_1, y_2, y_3 \geq 0$

There are three dual choice variables, although there are only two primal constraints.

(b) Using the new variable y_4, we can rewrite the dual as:

Maximize $\quad C^* = r_1y_1 + r_2y_4$

subject to $\quad a_{11}y_1 + a_{21}y_4 \leq c_1$

$\quad a_{12}y_1 + a_{22}y_4 \leq c_2$

and $\quad y_1 \geq 0$

Although y_2 and y_3 are nonnegative, the sign of y_4 is uncertain, because y_2 can exceed y_3, or vice versa.

(c) The statement is valid.

Exercise 20.2

1 The dual is

Minimize $\quad \pi^* = 16{,}000y_1 - 5y_2 + 4y_3$

subject to $\quad 800y_1 - y_2 \geq 1$

$\quad 4{,}000y_1 + y_3 \geq 6$

and $\quad y_1, y_2, y_3 \geq 0$

The π^* variable measures the number of potential customers (in thousands or some other units). The three dual choice variables represent, respectively, the number of potential customers per advertising dollar spent, per (required) radio spot, and per (available) television spot.

The coefficient for y_2 is negative because the firm is forced to sign up for a minimum of 5 radio spots, even if it may wish to take less.

2 The Lagrange-multiplier interpretation is $\bar{y}_i = \partial\bar{C}/\partial r_i$, which is a measure of how an increase in the ith nutrient requirement (i.e., a tightening of the ith primal constraint) changes the minimal total food cost (i.e., the optimal value of the primal objective function). This is obviously consistent with the interpretation of y_i as the imputed value of the ith nutrient.

Exercise 20.3

1 (a) Plot the points (2,5), (3,2) and (5,1), with K on the horizontal axis and L on the vertical axis.

(b) Connect the above three points by adjacent pairs. There is only a single kink, at (3,2).

2 No, it is not as efficient as A_2, because it requires as much capital as, but also more labor than, the second activity. Thus the fourth activity would be dominated.

3 (a) Yes. We can let $\begin{bmatrix} 5/2 \\ 7/2 \end{bmatrix} = \theta A_1 + (1 - \theta)A_2$, and find out whether such a number $0 \le \theta \le 1$ exists. It does; $\theta = \frac{1}{2}$. Thus this point is a convex combination, $\frac{1}{2}A_1 + \frac{1}{2}A_2$.

(b) Yes; this is $\frac{1}{3}A_1 + \frac{2}{3}A_2$. (c) Yes; this is $\frac{3}{4}A_2 + \frac{1}{4}A_3$.

4 (a) 3-space. (b) Yes.

(c) Pyramid, because the convex cone originates from convex combinations leading to flat surfaces rather than a curved wrap.

5 (a) The optimal output would be 3, because the new OK_0rL_0 rectangle would touch the highest possible isoquant at the point $3A_4$. Process 4 would be used exclusively.

(b) Since $\begin{bmatrix} K_0 \\ L_0 \end{bmatrix} = A_2 + 3A_3$, the optimal solution would consist of $\overline{Q}_2 = 1$ and $\overline{Q}_3 = 3$ (with $\overline{Q}_1 = \overline{Q}_4 = 0$). The optimal output would be $\overline{Q}_2 + \overline{Q}_3 = 4$.

6 If point r were located due north of point $4A_1$, the optimal solution would be $\overline{Q}_1 = 4$, with $\overline{Q}_2 = \overline{Q}_3 = \overline{Q}_4 = 0$. This time, although K_0 would be fully utilized, L_0 would not.

7 If the inputs available are, say, nK_1 and nL_1, we can attain the kink point of that particular isoquant associated with the output level $Q = nK_1/K_1 = nL_1/L_1 = n$. Now if capital alone (or labor alone) becomes available in an excess amount over nK_1 (or nL_1), that excess can be of no use, so that the output must remain at $Q = n$. Consequently, we can always take the minimum of the set of ratios $\{\frac{K}{K_1}, \frac{L}{L_1}\}$ as indicative of the output that we can produce.

Exercise 20.4

1 $\sum_{j=1}^{n} a_{0j}x_j \leq L_0$, or $A_0'x \leq L_0$.

2 If all activities are operated at the zero level (with complete inactivity), we will have $0A_1 + 0A_2 + \ldots + 0A_n = 0$. This last zero is a zero vector, and it means graphically the point of origin in the n-space.

3 The cone consists of all the points lying

(i) on or below the ray $\begin{bmatrix} 1 \\ 1 \end{bmatrix} Q_1$

(ii) on or above the ray $\begin{bmatrix} 2 \\ -1 \end{bmatrix} Q_2$

4 (a) The procedure for delineating the isolabor plane segment is similar to that of identifying the isoquant in Fig. 20.3. In the present input-output framework, each point on an activity ray [see Fig. 20.6(b)] indicates a particular level of operation of that activity (say, producing x_1). That point is therefore associated with a particular level of labor input. If the points that correspond to the labor input $L = 1$ on the three activity rays are, respectively, p_1, p_2, and p_3, then these latter points must be located on the unit isolabor plane segment. But so will also be the convex combinations of each of the pairs of points (p_1, p_2), (p_1, p_3), and (p_2, p_3), since each such combination would also require the same amount of labor ($L = 1$). Moreover, these convex combinations may themselves be further convex-combined to yield other points on the unit isolabor plane segment. Since, given three activity rays, the set of all such combinations is a solid triangle, the isolabor plane segment must be triangular in shape.

(b) With a_{01}, a_{02}, and a_{03} assumed to be constant, the isolabor plane segment for $L = 2$ is simply the set of all convex combinations generated by the three points $2p_1$, $2p_2$, and $2p_3$. That set is another triangular plane segment parallel to the one associated with $L = 1$. The same reasoning also applies for $L = 3$, and so forth.

CHAPTER 21

Exercise 21.1

1 The objective function generates a family of concentric circles with center at (0, 0). To minimize C, we move in the direction of (0, 0). Since the feasible region consists of the set of points on and above the rectangular hyperbola $x_1x_2 = 25$, the optimal solution is located where the rectangular hyperbola is tangent to one of the circles. To find the values of $\bar{x}_1$ and $\bar{x}_2$, we utilize two facts. First, those values must satisfy the equation

$$x_1x_2 = 25$$

Secondly, the circle and the rectangular hyperbola must have the same slope at the point of tangency. Since these slopes (which can be found by the implicit-function rule) are $-x_1/x_2$ (circle), and $-x_2/x_1$ (rectangular hyperbola), by equating them we get

$$x_1 = x_2$$

From the above twe equations, we obtain $(\bar{x}_1, \bar{x}_2) = (5, 5)$.

2 The objective function generates a family of concentric circles with center at (0, 2). To maximize π, we try to get to the largest possible circle. Since the feasible region consists of the set of points on or blow the line $5x_1 + 3x_2 = 15$ in the first quadrant, the optimal solution is $(\bar{x}_1, \bar{x}_2) = (3, 0)$.

3 The linear objective function generates a family of parallel straight lines with slope -1. The first constraint is equivalent to $x_2 \geq 9 - x_1^2$, so it requires us to pick the points on or above the parabola $x_2 = 9 - x_1^2$. The second constraint, equivalent to $x_1x_2 \leq 8$, confines us to the points on or below the rectangular hyperbola $x_1x_2 = 8$. Thus the feasible region consists of two disjoint parts. The optimal point that minimizes C is found to be $(\bar{x}_1, \bar{x}_2) = (3, 0)$.

4 The revenue function is $R = P_1x_1 + P_2x_2$, and the total-gross-profit function is $\pi = R - V_1x_1 - V_2x_2 = (P_1 - V_1)x_1 + (P_2 - V_2)x_2$. From the demand functions, we have $P_1 = \frac{a}{b} - \frac{1}{b}x_1$, and $P_2 = \frac{c}{d} - \frac{1}{d}x_2$. Thus the desired function is

$$\pi = (\frac{a}{b} - \frac{1}{b}x_1 - m - x_1)x_1 + (\frac{c}{d} - \frac{1}{d}x_2 - n - x_2^2)x_2$$

$$= (\frac{a}{b} - m)x_1 - (\frac{1}{b} + 1)x_1^2 + (\frac{c}{d} - n)x_2 - \frac{1}{d}x_2^2 - x_2^3$$

which is nonlinear.

5 The surface will be shaped like a vertically held ice-cream cone, with its tip resting on the point (4, 4) in the x_1x_2 base plane.

6 By introducing the dummy variable s, we can express the constraint as an equation: $x_1x_2 - s = 25$. Now let $x_1 \equiv u^2$; $x_2 \equiv v^2$, and $s \equiv w^2$. Then the problem can be reformulated in the classical mold:

Minimize $\quad C = u^4 + v^4$

subject to $\quad u^2v^2 - w^2 = 25$

where u, v and w do not have to be restricted to be nonnegative. To solve this problem, we write

$$Z = u^4 + v^4 + \lambda(25 - u^2v^2 + w^2)$$

with the following four equations as the first-order condition:

(a) $Z_\lambda = 25 - u^2v^2 + w^2 = 0$

(b) $Z_u = 4u^3 - 2\lambda uv^2 = 0$

(c) $Z_v = 4v^3 - 2\lambda u^2v = 0$

(d) $Z_w = 2\lambda w = 0$

From (b) and (c), we can get $2\lambda = 4u^3/uv^2$, and $2\lambda = 4v^3/u^2v$. When the two are equated, we find that $u^2/v^2 = v^2/u^2$, implying that $\bar{u} = \bar{v}$. Using this fact, we see from (b) or (c) that $\bar{\lambda} = 2$. Then from (d), it follows that $\bar{w} = 0$, so that (a) becomes $u^2v^2 = 25$, or $u^4 = v^4 = 25$, yielding $\bar{u}^2 = \bar{v}^2 = 5$, or by reverse substitution,

$$\bar{x}_1 = \bar{u}^2 = 5 \qquad \text{and} \qquad \bar{x}_2 = \bar{v}^2 = 5$$

This solution is identical with the one obtained earlier graphically.

Exercise 21.2

1 For the minimization problem, the necessary conditions become

(21.4') $f'(x_1) = 0$ and $x_1 > 0$

(21.5') $f'(x_1) = 0$ and $x_1 = 0$

(21.6') $f'(x_1) > 0$ and $x_1 = 0$

These can be condensed into the single statement

(21.7') $f'(x_1) \geq 0 \qquad x_1 \geq 0 \qquad \text{and} \qquad x_1 f'(x_1) = 0$

2 (a) Since y_i and $\partial Z/\partial y_i$ are both nonnegative, each of the m component terms in the summation expression must be nonnegative, and there is no possibility for any term to be cancelled out by another, the way (-3) cancels out (+3). Consequently, the summation expression can be zero if and only if every component term is zero. This is why the one-equation condition is equivalent to the m separate conditions taken together as a set.

(b) We can do the same for the conditions $x_j \dfrac{\partial Z}{\partial x_j} = 0$. This is because, for each j, $x_j \dfrac{\partial Z}{\partial x_j}$ must be nonpositive, so that no "cancellation" is possible.

3 The conditions $x_j \dfrac{\partial Z}{\partial x_j} = 0$ $(j = 1, 2, \ldots, n)$ can be condensed, and so can the conditions $y_i \dfrac{\partial Z}{\partial y_i} = 0$ $(i = 1, 2, \ldots, m)$.

4 The expanded version of (21.19) is:

$$\frac{\partial Z}{\partial x_j} = f_j - \sum_{i=1}^{m} y_i g_j^i \geq 0 \qquad x_j \geq 0 \qquad \text{and} \qquad x_j\left(f_j - \sum_{i=1}^{m} y_i g_j^i\right) = 0$$

$$\frac{\partial Z}{\partial y_i} = r_i - g^i(x_1, \ldots, x_n) \leq 0 \qquad y_i \geq 0$$

$$\text{and} \qquad y_i[r_i - g^i(x_1, \ldots, x_n)] = 0$$

$$(i = 1, 2, \ldots, m; \quad j = 1, 2, \ldots, n)$$

5 Maximize $-C = -f(x_1, \ldots, x_n)$

subject to $-g^1(x_1, \ldots, x_n) \leq -r_1$

$\ldots\ldots\ldots\ldots\ldots\ldots\ldots$

$-g^m(x_1, \ldots, x_n) \leq -r_m$

and $x_1, \ldots, x_n \geq 0$

With the Lagrangian function in the form of

$$Z = -f(x_1, \ldots, x_n) + \sum_{i=1}^{m} y_i[-r_i + g^i(x_1, \ldots, x_n)]$$

the Kuhn-Tucker conditions (21.18) yield

$$\frac{\partial Z}{\partial x_j} = -f_j + \sum_{i=1}^{m} y_i g_j^i \leq 0 \qquad x_j \geq 0 \qquad \text{and } x_j \frac{\partial Z}{\partial x_j} = 0$$

$$\frac{\partial Z}{\partial y_i} = -r_i + g^i(x_1, \ldots, x_n) \geq 0 \qquad y_i \geq 0 \qquad \text{and} \qquad y_i \frac{\partial Z}{\partial y_i} = 0$$

$$(i = 1, 2, \ldots, m; \; j = 1, 2, \ldots, n)$$

These are identical with the results in the preceding problem.

6 (a) $Z = (x_1 - 4)^2 + (x_2 - 4)^2 + y_1(5 - x_1 - x_2) + y_2(-6 + x_1) + y_3(-11 + 2x_2)$

$$\frac{\partial Z}{\partial x_1} = 2(x_1 - 4) - y_1 + y_2 \geq 0$$

$$\frac{\partial Z}{\partial x_2} = 2(x_2 - 4) - y_1 + 2y_3 \geq 0$$

$$\frac{\partial Z}{\partial y_1} = 5 - x_1 - x_2 \leq 0$$

$$\frac{\partial Z}{\partial y_2} = -6 + x_1 \leq 0$$

$$\frac{\partial Z}{\partial y_3} = -11 + 2x_2 \leq 0$$

plus the nonnegativity and complementary-slackness conditions

(b) Given $\bar{x}_1 = \bar{x}_2 = 4$, we have in the optimal solution

$$\frac{\partial Z}{\partial y_1} = -3 < 0 \qquad \frac{\partial Z}{\partial y_2} = -2 < 0 \qquad \frac{\partial Z}{\partial y_3} = -3 < 0$$

Thus, by complementary slackness, we can write $\bar{y}_1 = \bar{y}_2 = \bar{y}_3 = 0$.

(c) In the optimal solution, $\frac{\partial Z}{\partial x_1} = \frac{\partial Z}{\partial x_2} = 0$.

(d) All the Kuhn-Tucker conditions are satisfied.

Exercise 21.3

1 Since $\bar{x}_1$ and $\bar{x}_2$ are both nonzero, we may disregard (21.20), but (21.21) requires that:

$$6x_1(10 - x_1^2 - x_2)^2\, dx_1 + 3(10 - x_1^2 - x_2)^2\, dx_2 \leq 0$$

$$\text{and } -dx_1 \leq 0$$

The first inequality is automatically satisfied at the solution, and the second means that $dx_1 \geq 0$, with dx_2 free. Thus we may admit as a test vector, say, $(dx_1, dx_2) = (1, 0)$, which plots as an arrow pointing eastward from the solution point in Fig. 21.5. No qualifying arc can be found for this vector.

2 The constraint border is a circle with a radius of 1, and with its center at (0, 0). The optimal solution is at (1, 0). By (21.20), the test vectors must satisfy $dx_2 \geq 0$. By (21.21), we must have $2\bar{x}_1\, dx_1 + 2\bar{x}_2\, dx_2 = 2dx_1 \leq 0$. Thus the test vectors can only point towards due north, northwest, or due west. There does exist a qualifying arc for each such vector. (E.g., the constraint border itself can serve as a qualifying arc for the due-north test vector, as illustrated in the accompanying diagram.)

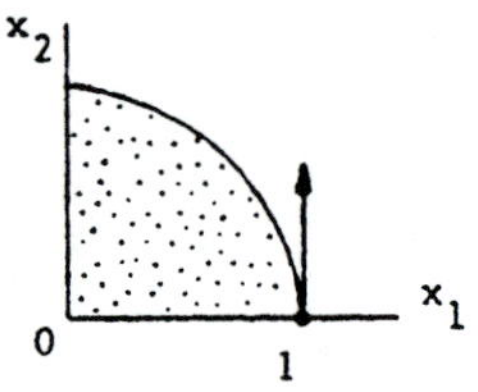

The Lagrangian function and the Kuhn-Tucker conditions are;

$$Z = x_1 + y_1(1 - x_1^2 - x_2^2)$$

$$\partial Z/\partial x_1 = 1 - 2y_1x_1 \leq 0$$

$$\partial Z/\partial x_2 = 1 - 2y_1x_2 \leq 0$$

$$\partial Z/\partial y_1 = 1 - x_1^2 - x_2^2 \geq 0$$

plus the nonnegativity and complementary-slackness conditions

Since $\bar{x}_1 = 1$, $\partial Z/\partial x_1$ should vanish; thus $\bar{y}_1 = 1/2$. This value of $\bar{y}_1$, together with the $\bar{x}_1$ and $\bar{x}_2$ values, satisfy all the Kuhn-Tucker conditions.

3 The feasible region consists of the points in the first quadrant lying on or below the curve $x_2 = x_1^2$. The optimal solution is at the point of origin, a cusp.

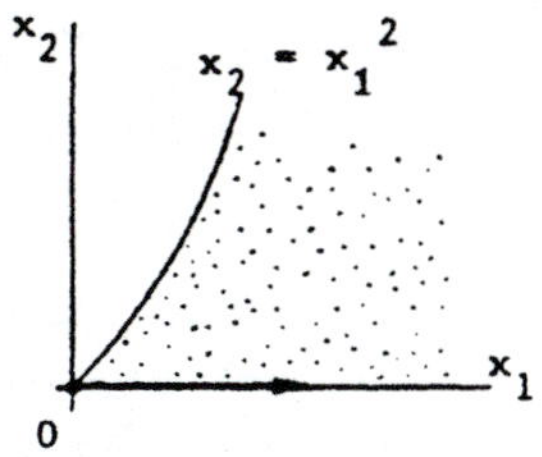

Since $\bar{x}_1 = \bar{x}_2 = 0$, the test vectors must satisfy $dx_1 \geq 0$ and $dx_2 \geq 0$, by (21.20). Moreover, (21.21) shows that we must have $2\bar{x}_1\, dx_1 - dx_2 = -dx_2 \geq 0$, or $dx_2 \leq 0$. The double requirement of $dx_2 \geq 0$ and $dx_2 \leq 0$ means that $dx_2 = 0$. Thus the test vectors must be horizontal, and pointing eastward (except for the null vector which does not point anywhere). Qualifying arcs clearly do exist for each such vector.

The Lagrangian function and the Kuhn-Tucker conditions are:

$$Z = x_1 + y_1(-x_1^2 + x_2)$$

$$\partial Z/\partial x_1 = 1 - 2y_1 x_1 \geq 0$$

$$\partial Z/\partial x_2 = y_1 \geq 0$$

$$\partial Z/\partial y_1 = -x_1^2 + x_2 \leq 0$$

plus the nonnegativity and complementary-slackness conditions

At (0, 0), the first and the third marginal conditions are duly satisfied. As long as we choose any value of $\bar{y}_1 \geq 0$, all the Kuhn-Tucker conditions are satisfied despite the cusp.

4 The global minimum is given by $(\bar{x}_1, \bar{x}_2) = (0, 0)$. Thus the test vectors must satisfy $dx_1 \geq 0$ and $dx_2 \geq 0$, by (21.20). Also, the first constraint being exactly satisfied, (21.21) requires that $(2\bar{x}_1 - 4)\, dx_1 + dx_2 = -4\, dx_1 + dx_2 \geq 0$. The latter implies the condition $dx_2/dx_1 \geq 4$, $(dx_1 \neq 0)$. Since the first constraint curve (a parabola) has a slope of 4 at (0, 0), all test vectors must be steeper than the parabola, so as to lie within F_1. Qualifying arcs do exist for all test vectors.

The Lagrangian function and the Kuhn-Tucker conditions are:

$$Z = 2x_1 + x_2 + y_1(-x_1^2 + 4x_1 - x_2) + y_2(-12 + 2x_1 + 3x_2)$$

$$\partial Z/\partial x_1 = 2 - 2y_1x_1 + 4y_1 + 2y_2 \geq 0$$

$$\partial Z/\partial x_2 = 1 - y_1 + 3y_2 \geq 0$$

$$\partial Z/\partial y_1 = -x_1^2 + 4x_1 - x_2 \leq 0$$

$$\partial Z/\partial y_2 = -12 + 2x_1 + 3x_2 \leq 0$$

plus the nonnegativity and complementary-slackness conditions

Since $\partial Z/\partial y_2 = -12$ at (0, 0), $\bar{y}_2$ must be zero. The top two marginal conditions then reduce to

$$2 + 4y_1 \geq 0 \qquad \text{and} \qquad 1 - y_1 \geq 0$$

The first of these is automatically satisfied when y_1 is nonnegative; the second requires that $\bar{y}_1 \leq 1$. With $0 \leq \bar{y}_1 \leq 1$, and $\bar{y}_2 = 0$, all the Kuhn-Tucker conditions are satisfied at (0, 0).

5 (a) $Z = x_1 + y_1[x_2 + (1 - x_1)^3]$

Complementary slackness requires that $\partial Z/\partial x_1$ vanish, but we actually find that, at the optimal solution (1, 0), $\partial Z/\partial x_1 = 1 - 3y_1(1 - x_1)^2 = 1$.

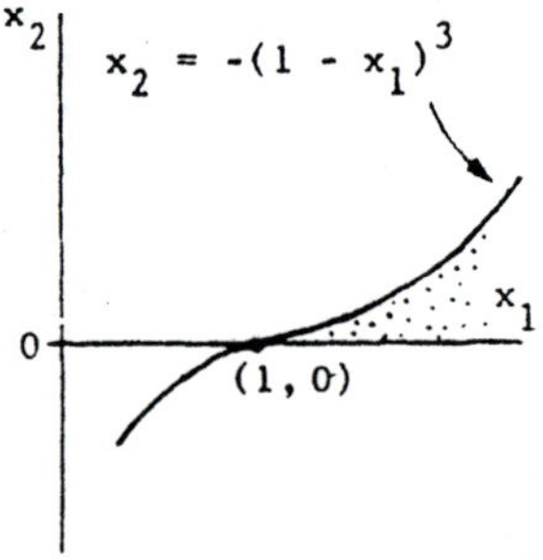

(b) $Z_0 = y_0x_1 + y_1[x_2 + (1 - x_1)^3]$

The Kuhn-Tucker conditions are:

$$\partial Z_0/\partial x_1 = y_0 - 3y_1(1 - x_1)^2 \geq 0$$

$$\partial Z_0/\partial x_2 = y_1 \geq 0$$

$$\partial Z_0/\partial y_1 = x_2 + (1 - x_1)^3 \leq 0$$

plus the nonnegativity and complementary-slackness conditions

By choosing $\bar{y}_0 = 0$ and $\bar{y}_1 \geq 0$, we can satisfy all of these conditions at the optimal solution.

Exercise 21.4

1 (a) Maximize $\quad -C = -F(x)$

subject to $\quad -G^i(x) \leq r_i \qquad (i = 1, 2, \ldots, m)$

and $\quad x \geq 0$

(b) $f(x) = -F(x)$, and $g^i(x) = -G^i(x)$.

(c) $F(x)$ should be convex, and $G^i(x)$ should be concave, in the nonnegative orthant.

(d) Given the minimization program: Minimize $C = F(x)$, subject to $G^i(x) \geq r_i$, and $x \geq 0$, if (a) F is differentiable and convex in the nonnegative orthant, (b) each G^i is differentiable and concave in the nonnegative orthant, and (c) the point $\bar{x}$ satisfies the Kuhn-Tucker minimum conditions (21.19), then $\bar{x}$ gives a global minimum of C.

2 When the sufficient conditions are satisfied, $F(x)$ is convex. Also, each $G^i(x)$ is concave. Thus, by (11.28), the set

$$S^{\geq} \equiv \{x \mid G^i(x) \geq r_i\}$$

is a (closed) convex set. The feasible region, being the intersection of the m closed convex sets $S_i^{\geq}$, $(i = 1, 2, \ldots, m)$, is itself a closed convex set. Thus the globality theorem applies in the minimization context too.

3 No. A unique saddle value should satisfy the strict inequality $Z(x, \bar{y}) < Z(\bar{x}, \bar{y}) < Z(\bar{x}, y)$ because uniqueness precludes the possibility of $Z(x, \bar{y}) = Z(\bar{x}, \bar{y})$ and $Z(\bar{x}, \bar{y}) = Z(\bar{x}, y)$.

4 (a) Applicable: $f(x)$ is linear and, hence, concave; and $g^1(x)$ is convex because it is a sum of convex functions.

(b) Applicable: $f(x)$ is convex; and $g^1(x)$ is linear and, hence, concave.

(c) Inapplicable: $f(x)$ is linear and may thus be considered as convex, but $g^1(x)$ is convex too, which violates condition (b) for the minimization problem.

Exercise 21.5

1 See Exercise 21.4-1; the reason is similar.

2 Sufficient conditions, not necessary conditions.

3 The function in (b) is mathematically acceptable; it is the only one that is quasiconcave.

4 (a) Yes. First, $g^1(x)$ and $g^2(x)$ are both differentiable and quasiconvex. Secondly, there does exist a point, such as (1, 4), that satisfies both constraints as strict inequalities. Thirdly, both $g^1(x)$ and $g^2(x)$ are convex. Thus the conditions in the constraint-qualification test are all satisfied.

(b) Yes. First, $g^1(x)$ and $g^2(x)$ are both differentiable and quasiconvex. (The function x_1x_2, like $K^{\alpha}L^{\beta}$, is quasiconcave; thus $-x_1x_2$ is quasiconvex.) Secondly, there is a point, such as (3, 4), that satisfies both constraints as strict inequalities. Thirdly, while condition (c-i) is <u>not</u> satisfied ($-x_1x_2$ is not convex in x_1 and x_2), condition (c-ii) <u>is</u> ($g_1^1 = g_2^1 = 1$, and $g_1^2 = -x_2 \neq 0$, $g_2^2 = -x_1 \neq 0$ at every point in the feasible region). Thus the conditions in the constraint-qualification test are again all satisfied.

Exercise 21.6

1 With $Z = U(x_1, \ldots, x_n) + y(B - P_1x_1 - \ldots - P_nx_n)$, the conditions are:

$$\frac{\partial Z}{\partial x_j} = U_j - yP_j \le 0 \qquad (j = 1, \ldots, n)$$

$$\frac{\partial Z}{\partial y} = B - P_1x_1 - \ldots - P_nx_n \ge 0$$

plus the nonnegativity and complementary-slackness conditions

2 With $Z = P_KK + P_LL + y(Q_0 - K^{\alpha}L^{\beta})$, the conditions are:

$$\frac{\partial Z}{\partial K} = P_K - y\alpha K^{\alpha-1}L^{\beta} \ge 0$$

$$\frac{\partial Z}{\partial L} = P_L - y\beta K^{\alpha}L^{\beta-1} \geq 0$$

$$\frac{\partial Z}{\partial y} = Q_0 - K^{\alpha}L^{\beta} \leq 0$$

plus the nonnegativity and complementary-slackness conditions

3 (a) Maximize $R = R(Q, A)$

subject to $C(Q) + A - R(Q, A) \leq -\pi_0 \quad (\pi_0 > 0)$

and $Q, A \geq 0$

(b) R must be concave, and C must be convex.

(c) R must be quasiconcave, and $C(Q) + A - R(Q, A)$ must be quasi-convex.

4 (a) Yes; yes.

(b) With $Z = x_1^2 + x_2^2 + y(2 - x_1 - x_2)$, the conditions are:

$$\frac{\partial Z}{\partial x_1} = 2x_1 - y \geq 0$$

$$\frac{\partial Z}{\partial x_2} = 2x_2 - y \geq 0$$

$$\frac{\partial Z}{\partial y} = 2 - x_1 - x_2 \leq 0$$

plus the nonnegativity and complementary-slackness conditions

The (0, 0) possibility can be dismissed because it violates the constraint.

The (0, +) possibility means $x_1 = 0$ and $x_2 > 0$. The fact that $x_1 = 0$ implies $\partial Z/\partial x_1 = -y \geq 0$, or $y \leq 0$. But $x_2 > 0$ implies $\partial Z/\partial x_2 = 0$ (by complementary slackness), yielding $y = 2x_2 > 0$. Hence this possibility involves a contradiction.

The (+, 0) possibility leads to a similar contradiction, because the roles of x_1 and x_2 in this problem are symmetrical.

The (+, +) possibility means (by complementary slackness) that $\partial Z/\partial x_1 = \partial Z/\partial x_2 = 0$, i.e., $2x_1 = y$, and $2x_2 = y$, and thus

$x_1 = x_2$. The positive sign of x_1 and x_2 also implies $y > 0$, so that $\partial Z/\partial y = 0$. Consequently, we have $2 - x_1 - x_2 = 0$, which yields $\bar{x}_1 = \bar{x}_2 = 1$.

5 (a) The distance from (0, 0) to any point (x_1, x_2) is

$$d = \sqrt{(x_1 - 0)^2 + (x_2 - 0)^2} = \sqrt{x_1^2 + x_2^2} > 0$$

The appropriate nonlinear program is

$$\begin{aligned} &\text{Minimize} && d = \sqrt{x_1^2 + x_2^2} \\ &\text{subject to} && x_1 + x_2 \geq 2 \\ &\text{and} && x_1, x_2 \geq 0 \end{aligned}$$

(b) The only difference is the objective function. Since d is a monotonic transformation of $C = x_1^2 + x_2^2$ (i.e., the larger C is, the larger d will be), the solution $(\bar{x}_1, \bar{x}_2)$ that minimizes C also minimizes d. So we also have $\bar{x}_1 = \bar{x}_2 = 1$ here.

(c) $\bar{d} = \sqrt{1 + 1} = \sqrt{2}$.